INTERNATIONAL RESCUE
Thunderbirds

Haynes®

TB1–TB5, Tracy Island and associated rescue vehicles

Agents' Technical Manual

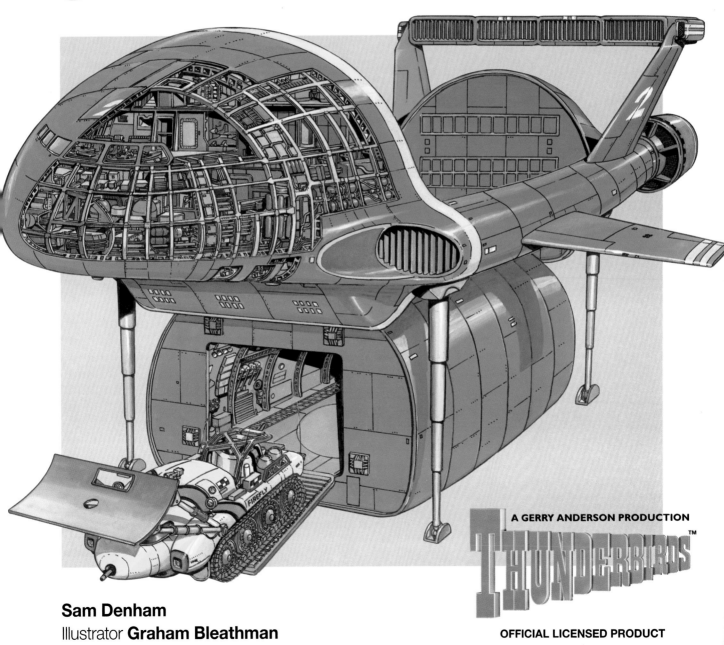

A GERRY ANDERSON PRODUCTION

THUNDERBIRDS™

Sam Denham

Illustrator **Graham Bleathman**

OFFICIAL LICENSED PRODUCT

CONTENTS

Author's note

When Thunderbirds was first screened in 1965, none of the programme's production team could have imagined that the series they had created would still be held in great affection by viewers around the world almost half a century later, or that the futuristic world they had brought to the screen might be the subject of a manual such as this.

But thanks to the care and attention with which the team visualized the 21st Century adventures of the Tracy family and their Thunderbirds machines, the series has enjoyed continued popularity following re-screenings and video and DVD releases. In turn this has allowed new generations to experience the incredible exploits of International Rescue, and to marvel at the technical ingenuity of the machines and gadgets featured in their missions. As a result of this remarkable vision, it has been possible to produce this detailed guide to the incredible world of Thunderbirds.

Since the optimistic days of the 1960s, however, technology has inevitably moved on and although many of the scientific advances anticipated in the series are still technically believable, others have been superseded or proved unworkable. Equally, the pressures of producing a series of television films on budget and to a tight deadline has at times resulted in lapses in continuity and the dependence on a certain amount of dramatic licence. Over the years various differing back stories have also been created to give depth to the characters, many of these accounts being contradictory. This has made it a challenging task to completely rationalise every aspect of the series. In producing this book we have endeavoured to fuse these various elements together to create a believable vision of a late 21st Century world, but this has not always been possible without creating a few short-circuits.

Despite any resulting inconsistencies, we believe the principles behind the programme still hold strong, and with the advent of the digital age are perhaps even more relevant in a world increasingly reliant on science and technology. For this extraordinary vision we must thank the inventive talents of producers Gerry and Sylvia Anderson and their team of writers, artists and technicians, to whom this book is dedicated.

I nternational Rescue was formed for one reason, and one reason alone: to provide a means of rescue when all other methods have failed. To bring this dream to reality my five sons and I have worked tirelessly with our uniquely talented scientific advisor, known to us all as 'Brains', to create a rescue organisation that can call on the latest technological advances to anticipate potential global disasters and carry out otherwise impossible rescue missions with the aid of highly specialised equipment.

The creation and effective testing of our organisation would clearly have been inconceivable without the aid of a worldwide network of trusted associates to provide logistical support and assist in supplying vital components and resources. Without this help the design and construction of the machines and installations we require would have presented an insurmountable obstacle.

Now that our combined efforts have led these plans to become a working reality, our continued challenge is to maintain the effective day-to-day running of International Rescue at maximum efficiency. To enable us to do so we have prepared this detailed manual to issue to all field agents. This contains the essential in-depth working knowledge that any local agent might require should they be called on to provide mission assistance or technical aid in effecting mechanical repairs to our craft and equipment. In it can be found detailed mechanical diagrams and technical instructions to fully understand the inner workings of International Rescue's fabulous Thunderbirds machines, launch installations and ancillary vehicles.

It is, of course, vital that this manual and its contents should remain completely confidential, as the information it contains could be used to endanger lives if it were to fall into the wrong hands. It is recommended that it be kept securely locked in a Cahelium-lined security safe at all times.

In conclusion, I would like to take this opportunity to thank all our agents around the world for their continued dedicated support for our organisation and its aims, and to remind them not to forget the code of International Rescue – 'Never Give In at Any Cost'

Jeff Tracy

Jeff Tracy
Commander in Chief, International Rescue

THIS IS 2065

The late 21st Century has seen the world transformed by incredible advances in technological development.

In all walks of human life scientists and engineers have been astounding mankind with new marvels of mechanical ingenuity and scientific innovation. These endeavours have helped create a world that is now largely at peace and is becoming increasingly united as nations work together to provide a secure future for the planet's inhabitants.

The formulation of new fuels, the widespread use of atomic power and the increased application of automation have been at the forefront of this new age of technical achievement, revolutionising many industrial processes and streamlining international transportation systems. The resulting effect of these advances can be seen around the globe in all fields of human enterprise.

On land new cities have been built, either as conventional suburban developments, showcased by the award-winning radiating layout of North America's Spoke City, or by taking tower block construction to new heights as initiated with the multi-purpose Thompson Tower sky-town project. Existing cities have also been redeveloped and modernised with integrated overhead transportation networks replacing

outdated sub-surface systems. In New York the scale of inner city redevelopment has resulted in the regeneration of entire areas of Manhattan Island , incorporating plans to preserve the Empire State Building as a historic monument by physically relocating the entire building in one piece to a new site.

New technologies are also constantly being developed to supply the food needs of the world's population. Pioneers in this field are the great agri-engineering combines, among them those which have since grown into the Tracy Corporation, the Kansas based civil engineering and aerospace giant. This company is a leading developer of highly automated crop management roto-cultivators controlled by its global monitoring network of weather satellites. These are being put to use in Australia and North Africa where large tracts of previously arid land have been given new life through the development of atomic irrigation and desalinisation plants. Experiments are also ongoing elsewhere into accelerated growth processes to enhance crop and livestock yields, while new sources of food are being sought from strains of oceanic sea-fungi - although this is currently only suitable for use as pet food. Forestry has also been revolutionised with sustainable areas of rainforest now being cultivated for further re-use by giant mobile logging and processing plants, designed to improve efficiency and increase wood product output.

New technology has brought continents closer together through the building of new and improved road networks and super highways linked by ambitious mountain cuttings and multi-span suspension bridges. These highways can now be built at previously impossible speeds due to the introduction of self-contained mobile road construction plants, such as those operated by the Gray and Houseman company in Asia and the Trans-Australia Corporation. In addition to new road infra-structure, international rail, shipping and aircraft

development has now enabled man to travel further, faster and in more comfort than ever before. Conventional ground based monorail systems have in recent years been super-ceded by suspended rail networks capable of greater speed. These are now operational in Europe with the Transcontinental Rocket and other express services linking Western and Eastern European capitals with the Middle East through government backed schemes, while private investment has seen the same technology introduced in North America.

The oceans too can now be crossed faster than ever before, and using less manpower, thanks to continued development of the international hover liner services first introduced in the 2020's, and the pioneering of new three man crew cargo vessel operating systems. But it is in the world of aviation that the greatest progress has been made. The inauguration of the new hypersonic Fireflash fleet by Air Terrainean has provided international travellers with a means of flying at speeds approaching Mach 5 and at heights in excess of 100,000 feet. This has led to the reduction of flying times from London to Australia to under five hours. The accident record of short haul subsonic flight is also constantly being improved, with revolutionary new safety features currently rumoured to be under consideration for introduction by Atlantic Airlines in their latest aircraft.

The growth of advanced new transportation systems is a primary indicator of the new developments in fuel and power generation processes. The ongoing exploration into all possible sources of new energy has seen efficient low emission fuels being synthesised by the Superon company, while the tapping of vast undersea gas reserves in the Atlantic by Seascape class generation drilling rigs has released new energy potential from the sea bed. Sea water itself has even been exploited to produce rocket fuel with the perfection of a new conversion formula that remains a closely guarded secret due to its potentially hazardous environmental impact. This new fuel has however already been deemed reliable enough to power a new manned mission to the Sun, enabling vital experiments to be conducted into analysing the chemical composition of solar prominences. It is hoped that this mission will help unlock the further potential of solar based power generation, in combination with attempts that are currently being made to harness the Sun's energy through the use of solar ray heat converters.

The Sun Probe project also perfectly encapsulates two areas in which the greatest technological progress has been made in recent years. In the use of automated launch systems Sun Probe highlights how , with advances in computerisation, only a minimal launch team is now required to supervise the complex preparation and monitoring of such a venture, which in turn has resulted in the development of satellite rocket launch programmes that can be controlled by just one person.

This new era of electronic mastery has seen automation applied in many other ways, allowing even the most complex vehicle or installation to be controlled by two or three suitably trained personnel. The credit for much of this work must go to two men - Wilbur Dandridge, the visionary head of Gazelle Automation, whose aim to introduce automated systems into every home and workplace has transformed everyday life around the world - and Jim Lucas, design genius in chief at Robotics International, who has devised new and sophisticated control systems for a wide range of applications, from ambulatory security drones and multi-story car stacking auto parks to the latest line of mechanised mobile forestry processors.

Apart from showcasing advances in automation technology, Project Sun Probe can also claim to be at the forefront of man's latest attempts to venture beyond Earth and investigate the mysteries of outer space. With the Moon

conquered, the next target is Mars, and already a Martian Space Probe mission has been authorised using conventional rocket technology. But these methods will shortly be outmoded with the construction at America's Glenn Field facility of Zero X, a revolutionary horizontally launched rocket craft fitted with detachable lifting bodies. This interplanetary giant will enable a five man mission to reach Mars in under three months and by means of a detachable tracked excursion vehicle will provide its occupants with the ability to carry out detailed surveys of the planet's surface.

Closer to home, space technology has now become part of every day life, with the rapid growth of trans-global satellite networks. This is most prominently noticeable in the broadcast media and communications industries. World TV, NTBS and the Trans American TV Network are now able to broadcast programmes around the globe with satellite signals boosted by ground based tele-relay stations standardised in the UK by the Skycontrol towers provided by the British Telecommunications Company. The creation of global media celebrities cast in the mould of such newscasters as Eddie Kerr and Ned Cook has however led to a less desirable form of space enterprise by those wishing to cash in on the satellite 'gold rush' through loopholes in current space use regulations. This has seen an alarming increase in unregulated 'pirate' satellite stations launched from independent states whose governments are not signatories of the World Space Exploration convention. These rogue satellite operations risk disrupting regulated orbital traffic and International Space Control is seeking new powers to outlaw such ventures before serious consequences result.

In addition to regulating commercial satellite operators, International Space Control also co-ordinates military satellite activity sanctioned by the united world powers. With the gradual handover of sovereign nation state military forces to provisional world government control, the military satellite

network of manned space observatories and Surveillance Platform Intelligence satellites have begun to play an integral role in controlling international military operations and monitoring the activities of unaligned independent states. ISC designated networks can also be accessed by global security forces and police departments in their fight against world-wide criminal elements. It is these trans-national security uses to which the latest space-age technology is being put that underlines one of the ongoing concerns faced by our otherwise peaceful world.

Although levels of crime have significantly decreased in recent years, wrong-doers still operate in many levels of society. From old fashioned safe-breakers and opportunistic con-men, to technologically sophisticated criminal organisations - among the most feared being the notorious Erdman Gang - criminal deviancy can take many forms, with shadowy international master villains proving the most elusive foes. This lawless activity is often sponsored by the same rogue nations that have declined to join the member states of the United World Council, whose security and police services face a continuing battle to protect the majority of Earth's law abiding citizens.

Aside from such retrogressive criminality, the world might otherwise appear to be enjoying the fruits of a man-made technological paradise, secure in the knowledge that international authorities can deal with any potential threat to normal life. But this sense of security might far too easily be taken for granted, and in extreme cases may even be dangerously misplaced. However carefully nations and industrial concerns might develop new means of benefiting mankind, an element of risk inevitably exists in any new venture, and even the most stringent safeguards can prove useless and ineffective. Whatever care is taken to anticipate the inherent weaknesses present in any new scientific

process or mechanical device, design flaws, technical failure, deliberate sabotage or even simple human error could result in unforeseeable dangers, while the effect of natural forces in any given situation can also be impossible to equate. It may seem unthinkable in our late 21st Century world, but even the safest and most thoroughly tested of new generation atomic engines might suffer from catastrophic malfunction. In extreme cases the consequences of such technological breakdowns or scientific short-comings might result in chaos and disaster, giving rise to potentially life threatening scenarios which conventional rescue services might prove incapable of coping with.

It is for this reason that a group of committed and experience men and women decided to gather together to form an ultra-secret organisation dedicated to providing a means of rescue in otherwise impossible circumstances. Under a leading industrialist and ex-astronaut's visionary leadership, and with the incredible technical ingenuity of one of the world's most brilliant scientific geniuses, a fully equipped multi-task response unit has been formed. Capable of reaching potential danger zones around the world at incredible speed, boasting the latest life-saving devices, and manned by highly skilled operators, the unit's fleet of vehicles have been designated the codename 'Thunderbirds', while the organisation itself has become known as a byword for global emergency assistance - International Rescue.

NOTE: Subsequent to the initial preparation of this data file, International Rescue has seen active engagement in numerous rescue missions around the world, demonstrating the vital need for its services. Details of selected actions can be found in supplementary mission files attached at the end of this manual.

LAUNCHING THE DREAM

Having spent over two decades building up his Tracy Corporation combine from a humble agricultural machinery manufacturer to a globally successful aerospace, engineering and construction empire, billionaire ex-astronaut Jeff Tracy could have retired and lived a life of luxury. But for some years he had been becoming increasingly conscious of the dangerously hazardous shortcomings of man-made technology, and the inadequate provision of specialised global rescue resources. This awareness was brought painfully close to home with the death of his wife in a tragic accident that could have been prevented with the help of suitable rescue equipment.

Through his work in engineering and construction, Jeff had also become aware of the development of new mechanical techniques and scientific processes that in the wrong hands

could endanger life. The solution was obvious - combine his desire to help others facing life threatening danger, with his knowledge of advances in science and technology, to create a super secret rescue organisation that could provide help in emergencies when all other methods had failed. So he took the bold decision to devote the vast fortune he had amassed to making this dream a reality for the benefit of mankind.

Reasoning that he would need to establish a well concealed operations base to house such an organisation, in addition to a plausible cover story to explain his withdrawal from day to day company life, Jeff could not believe his luck when geological surveys carried out by the Tracy Corporation revealed deposits of the rare super strong mineral ore Cahelium X in the strata of a group of remote Pacific islands. What could be

Commander in Chief
International Rescue
Jeff Tracy

AREA OF SPECIALISATION
Command and control of International Rescue operations

BACKGROUND
Brought up on a highly mechanised Kansas wheat farm, Jeff Tracy soon developed an interest in the complex agricultural technology employed to maximise crop production, and after service in the US military, which saw him rise to the rank of Colonel before his recruitment as a lunar mission astronaut for the International Space Agency, he returned to farming to build up an agricultural equipment manufacturing company. This rapidly grew into the successful trans-global Tracy Construction and Aerospace Corporation, enabling Jeff to secretly fund the creation of International Rescue, following the tragic death of his wife.

PERSONAL CHARACTERISTICS
Determined and compassionate, Jeff has the ability to remain calm and clear-headed in the time of any crisis, seeking a practical course of action that will provide the best possible solution to any problem. He cares strongly about his commitment to help others and is a firm but fair father.

a more natural location for a retired billionaire ex-astronaut to build a paradise retreat ? And with its remote location, unique mineral resources and a labyrinth of underground caverns, the once volcanic mass of rock would provide an ideal platform from which to launch his dream organisation. The outcrop and a neighbouring island were speedily purchased, and work quickly commenced to build a lavish villa and guest quarters. Here Jeff could gather his forces to plan and co-ordinate his grand design.

When his plan to create a global specialised rescue team was first conceived, Jeff knew that he would be dependent on the support of a group of trusted colleagues. The organisational and technical challenges his scheme posed, and the need for utter secrecy would test the mental abilities of the best international experts, but thanks to the varied range of world-wide contacts Jeff had built up during his years in industry and military service, the task of recruiting a suitably qualified and dedicated team of helpers proved relatively simple. With their specialised knowledge and practical design input plans were drawn up to make his ambitious dreams a reality.

Money being no object thanks to the immense personal fortune Jeff had accrued from his ownership of the Tracy Corporation, and with the same company also capable of providing cover for much of the manufacturing and experimental testing of the specialised new machinery his organisation required, work quickly progressed. Using automated methods pioneered by his old associate Wilbur Dandridge, construction could also be carried out by a minimal workforce, helping to reduce security risks, while new fuel and propulsion methods were developed by a team led by Sir Jeremy Hodge. With his contacts in Europe, Sir Jeremy also arranged for the secret manufacture of certain vital components on the continent.

To assist him in the supervision of his visionary plan, Jeff called on his five sons, all experienced pilots in their own field,

who would ultimately be responsible for carrying out rescue missions. One obstacle still remained however. It was soon realised that no-one in his team possessed the unique innovative vision required to design rescue craft advanced enough to fulfil all the requirements demanded of them. In the face of this seemingly insurmountable problem plans ground to a halt while Jeff instigated a search for a suitably talented genius.

After almost giving up hope, Jeff's quest at last met with success when one of his contacts suggested he should attend a talk being given at the annual scientific congress being held in Paris. In a small lecture hall, well away from the main complex, Jeff immediately recognised the incredible scientific genius of

the nervous young speaker, a scientist known to everyone as 'Brains'. Taking the stammering specialist to one side after his talk, Jeff briefly outlined his plans. To his grateful satisfaction, 'Brains' enthusiastically agreed to join Jeff's team. With custom built facilities on the newly christened 'Tracy Island', Jeff's protégé could focus all his mental abilities on engineering a fleet of craft that could demonstrate his innovative design theories while meeting the exacting requirements his new benefactor demanded. The various craft had to fly faster, carry more payload, dive deeper, and travel further into space, than any similar vehicles already in existence, while at the same time being more efficient and reliable.

Applying his extraordinary talents to the challenge, Brains proved Jeff's faith had not been misplaced by devising new mechanical processes and construction materials to create five uniquely tailored miracle machines. Each would be powered by the most advanced propulsion systems and be packed with life saving devices. Most importantly, each vehicle would also be equipped with revolutionary anti-detection equipment light years ahead of the latest word in military stealth capability. With the designs immediately approved, a construction programme was initiated at the secret automated facility that Jeff had set up in a seemingly abandoned Tracy Corporation construction plant, with the craft being subjected to ongoing testing by their prospective pilots.

With the manufacture of the organisation's main rescue craft underway, Brains then turned his attention to the

specialised ancillary vehicles that the team would require. To save time and resources, and in the same way that he had specified the utilisation of readily available component parts in the construction of the main Thunderbirds craft wherever possible, Brains employed a similar technique to create task specific field equipment. By combining commercially available traction units with ingenious purpose built devices a wide variety of rescue vehicles could be efficiently constructed in a short space of time. These ancillary vehicles would also provide Brains with the opportunity to test out new materials and power systems, and develop experimental technology. Many of the processes involved are still highly secret, although commercial applications have not been ruled out in some cases. Revolutionary progress with gravity compensation generators, presently only suitable for lightweight vehicles, looks particularly promising, with the future prospect of their being installed in much larger craft.

As construction of the operational hardware essential for rescue missions continued, and while his sons undertook a rigorous training programme to focus their physical and mental skills, Jeff directed his attentions to building up International Rescue's world-wide network of agents. These agents would be strategically positioned in locations around the globe to provide a vital source of local information and operational support. They would be responsible for ensuring and maintaining the supply of essential material resources and mechanical components and could also engage in covert mission back-up action. Each would

be equipped with deceptively innocent looking gadgets and concealed communication devices, enabling them to operate in complete secrecy.

Realising that a top class agent with proven expertise in international espionage might provide invaluable guidance in running such a network, Jeff made discreet enquiries among contacts in military intelligence. One name kept being whispered. A glamorous British aristocrat who led a jet-set life as a journalist and fashion model might not be all she seemed. An invitation to an exclusive New York gallery opening gave Jeff the chance to view the fabulous society beauty at close quarters. It seemed incredible that such an apparently frivolous creature could be a resourceful undercover agent. So with Brains' help, Jeff devised a plan to put her to the test. It immediately became transparently obvious that he was dealing with no ordinary international super-model. His test passed with flying colours, and her abilities as a special agent proven, Jeff suggested that they should join forces. Intrigued and fascinated by his challenging proposition Lady Penelope Creighton-Ward became International Rescue's London Agent. The worldwide network was now complete.

At last, with every tri-circuit contact tested, every atomic motor primed, and all his team in place, Jeff Tracy's incredible organisation was ready for launch. Whatever the circumstances, whoever the victim and wherever the distress message should come from, International Rescue was ready to answer the call.

TRACY ISLAND

Situated in a remote sector of the central Pacific Ocean, midway between Australia and South America, Tracy Island appears to the outside world as an almost barren rock.

The Round House: a unique architectural structure built above a sunken Japanese garden, the Round House provides accommodation for island guests.

Tracy Villa: built to Jeff Tracy's personal design, the island's main residence is situated on a plateau on the northern side of the island.

Swimming pool: surrounded by palm trees, the island's outdoor swimming pool provides an idyllic setting for relaxation.

Cliff House: further guest accommodation and leisure facilities can be found in the concrete canopied Cliff House.

Runway: the palm tree lined runway provides the Tracy family and guests with a landing strip for their personal aircraft.

Communications mast: the remote location of Tracy Island requires a communications mast for contact with the outside world.

Senior Household Advisor
Grandma

AREA OF SPECIALISATION
Non-active observational duties only.

BACKGROUND
Having lived for most of her life in Kansas, where she and her husband Grant brought up Jeff, their only son, 'Grandma' relocated to southern California shortly after the Tracy Corporation opened its head office and main aerospace plant in the area. Situated near the border with New Mexico, and a short drive away from the Parola Sands raceway, her new home allowed her to keep a close eye on Jeff and his sons following the death of her daughter-in-law. With the family now established on Tracy Island, she has joined them to help supervise the household.

PERSONAL CHARACTERISTICS
Although sharp-witted and shrewd, with an active interest in world history and geography inspired by tales told by her globe-trotting mother, 'Grandma' does not share her son's faith in modern technology. This is demonstrated by her preference for traditional home cooking methods, rather than 'new-fangled' atomic techniques.

Formed as a result of seismic shifts in the ocean bed during the late Triassic age, approximately 200 million years ago, the island and its near neighbour Mateo are peaks of a sub-aquatic ridge that stretches east across the Pacific tectonic plate to its convergence with the Nazca and Antarctic plates. Now completely dormant, both islands were once volcanically active and are internally honeycombed with vast lava-formed chambers linked by a network of extinct vent channels. On the southern side of the island at sea level these form a network of cavernous grottoes, which are reputed to be the home of an elusive species of water mamba. The geological composition of the island's rock strata is also rich in valuable minerals, including sought after deposits of the ultra-rare Cahelium X.

Following Jeff Tracy's purchase of the island in the early 2060s, work quickly commenced to create an idyllic self-contained luxury retreat, indicating to the casual visitor that Tracy Island was nothing more than a lavish millionaire's paradise where the Tracy family could live a life of luxury oblivious to everyday reality. After construction of an airstrip leading from the northern edge of the island to the cliff edge of a small plateau, well placed to catch the dramatic Pacific sunsets, work started on a streamlined two-storey villa to Jeff's personal design. Built on an outcrop of rock overlooking a palm-fringed apron, which offered the perfect location for a kidney shaped swimming pool, the villa quickly took shape. Additional accommodation was also planned and constructed to provide guest quarters and leisure facilities. This consists of the Round House, a cantilevered doughnut-shaped residence built above a sunken circular oriental garden and accessed by a path running to the east of the main house, and the Cliff House, a jutting two-storey construction built into a cleft of rock situated above the landward end of the island's runway and topped with a domed concrete canopy. Internal lift and moving walkway systems link the Cliff House and Tracy Villa with a small hangar entrance built into the base of the cliff. A further internal travelway connects to a converted ocean-side cave which acts as a boathouse for the family's various seagoing craft.

TRACY ISLAND INTERIORS

To further sustain the façade of opulent extravagance Jeff believed it essential that his island home should project to innocent guests, its tasteful interior design incorporates every conceivable modern comfort.

A spacious lounge forms the focus of the main building, with family bedrooms and a small laboratory workshop on the same floor, all fitted with the latest audio and visual systems, including micro-layer flat screen TVs and total surround audio players. The same building also houses a modern kitchen and family dining room fitted with the latest model atomic cooker.

From the lower level, access can be made to a complex of leisure facilities built into the island's labyrinth of caves. A gym, shooting range, billiard room, a small cinema, a music room and an indoor pool are just a few of the amenities that the Tracy family can enjoy during moments of relaxation. These complement the natural resources the island offers for such outdoor pursuits as deep-sea diving, fishing, rock climbing and beach games.

Household Manager
Kyrano

AREA OF SPECIALISATION
Tracy Island domestic supervision.

BACKGROUND
Born in Malaya, Kyrano was the eldest son of a wealthy land owner, but on his father's death he was cheated of his rightful inheritance by his vicious, and reportedly paranormally gifted, half-brother. Turning his back on worldly possessions, Kyrano began a new life with his young daughter in a remote coastal region of Indo-China, where he helped save the life of crashed test pilot Jeff Tracy. In gratitude, Jeff found Kyrano a job at the Kennedy Space Centre's synthetic food development plant, allowing his daughter to receive the benefits of the best American education. Moving to London, and then Paris, while his daughter continued her education in Europe, Kyrano became an advisor at Kew Gardens and then head chef at the Paris Hilton, before rejoining the Tracy family to run their island household.

The décor of the main house reflects Jeff's taste in oriental design and culture. He developed this passion during several months recuperating in a remote area of Indo-China as a result of crash landing an experimental aircraft while on a proving flight. Another legacy of this enforced period of recovery came with his meeting Kyrano, who with his young daughter Tin-Tin was responsible for saving Jeff's life. Becoming a loyal friend and helper, together with Jeff's mother – known to all simply as 'Grandma' – Kyrano is now responsible for the domestic management of Tracy Island, while his daughter has recently completed an international education in science and technology, having shown a youthful gift for the subject.

In addition to Kyrano's duties as household manager, he is also responsible for supervising the island's supply of fresh food and water. Apart from being a natural source of tropical fruit and vegetables, one of the island's caverns has been converted into a subterranean hydroponics plant, supplied by fresh water springs supplemented by a compact sea water desalinisation processor. Combined with a extensive deep frozen food stores, this allows the island to be virtually self sufficient.

PERSONAL CHARACTERISTICS
Normally quiet, placid and philosophical, Kyrano is fiercely protective of his role as manager of Tracy Island, and will not allow any interference with his duties. He is also known to suffer from mysterious mental attacks, during which he can be found writhing on the floor and muttering incoherently. Despite the best medical treatment, no reason has been discovered to explain these alarming trance-like fits.

TRACY LOUNGE

Located on the west-facing side of the villa and overlooking the palm-shaded swimming pool, the Tracy lounge is the focus of the family home.

Accessed by a smaller reception room leading off a central hallway, the lounge is spacious and well lit with angled French windows along one wall opening onto a full-length balcony from the split-level floor space.

In the far corner, diagonally opposite the main entrance, is Jeff Tracy's desk and work station. Behind the desk are shelves lined with books and personal mementoes, surrounding a video monitor built into a compact electronic control unit and communication post. Originally mounted on twin supports prior to recent redecoration, the desk could be raised to the ceiling when not in use - but as this has proved rarely to be the case it has been replaced with a larger, conventionally supported version. This lacks the flip top feature of the original which initially housed an electronic keypad and printer.

Technical and Administrative Assistant
Tin-Tin

AREA OF SPECIALISATION
Investigative science and system management

BACKGROUND
The daughter of Jeff Tracy's trusted aide Kyrano, Tin-Tin grew up with the Tracy family while her father worked for the International Space Agency. Showing an early aptitude for science, Tin-Tin studied at various educational institutes in America and Europe gaining advanced degrees in mathematics and engineering. By an extraordinary turn of fate she was caught up in International Rescue's first mission when the Fireflash aircraft she was travelling in was subjected to sabotage.

PERSONAL CHARACTERISTICS
Tin-Tin has a sweet and attractive personality, and like her father she is extremely loyal. However, unlike her father she has a taste for adventure and is an expert skier and pilot.

Providing extra shade at sunset, a large screen depicting an oriental warrior is positioned to the right hand side of the desk, while on the wall to the desk's left is a full-length portrait of the lunar mission rocket that carried Jeff to the moon in the early 2050s. Immediately next to the painting are wall-mounted lamps providing illumination to compensate for the lack of natural light on this side of the lounge. Directly facing Jeff's desk, to the left of the room's main entrance, visitors will see portraits of his five sons in everyday casual attire. Another portrait, strategically placed to greet visitors, captures the elegant beauty of international fashion model Lady Penelope Creighton Ward, a close personal friend of the Tracy family.

Furnished throughout with comfortable sofas and easy chairs created by the world's leading furniture designers, the room exudes an Eastern theme with oriental ornaments and artwork prominently displayed. Pride of place, however, goes to a white grand piano, a gift from Jeff to his late wife, which is now mainly played by the musically gifted Virgil Tracy.

But in reality, like the rest of the Tracy's isolated island paradise, the outward appearance of the stylish lounge is merely a carefully conceived illusion, masking the real purpose of the Tracy's apparently idyllic existence. At the touch of a button, the casually dressed portraits are replaced by alternative images of the five Tracy sons in their International Rescue uniforms, the portraits doubling as communication screens allowing direct visual contact with each son, incoming calls being indicated by flashing ocular warning lights. To make or receive calls, an ornamental ashtray on Jeff's desk flips back to reveal a hidden microphone, while strategically concealed hangar access transit systems combine to effectively transform the lounge into a launch control and mission command centre for the Thunderbirds craft. From behind his desk Jeff can now supervise his organisation's operations, monitoring reports from the rescue zone and arranging additional mission support. From an area of tranquil relaxation, the lounge has now revealed itself to be the hub of the International Rescue team.

TRANSIT SYSTEMS

Behind Tracy Island's placid façade, the extent of International Rescue's conversion of the remote rocky outcrop is truly astonishing. A complex network of launch bays, laboratories, power plants and service tunnels provides storage and maintenance facilities for a fleet of primary rescue vehicles and additional specialised equipment.

Transit systems

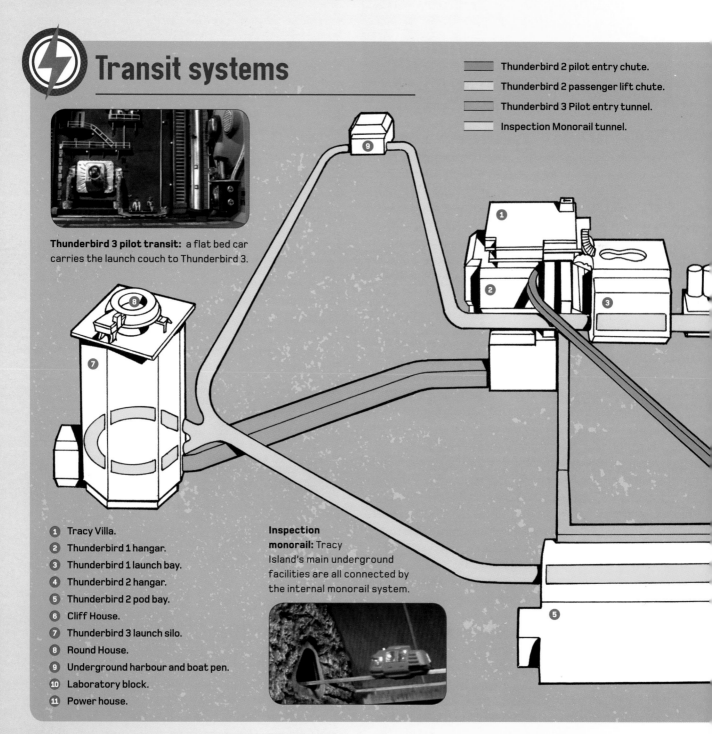

Thunderbird 2 pilot entry chute.

Thunderbird 2 passenger lift chute.

Thunderbird 3 Pilot entry tunnel.

Inspection Monorail tunnel.

Thunderbird 3 pilot transit: a flat bed car carries the launch couch to Thunderbird 3.

① Tracy Villa.
② Thunderbird 1 hangar.
③ Thunderbird 1 launch bay.
④ Thunderbird 2 hangar.
⑤ Thunderbird 2 pod bay.
⑥ Cliff House.
⑦ Thunderbird 3 launch silo.
⑧ Round House.
⑨ Underground harbour and boat pen.
⑩ Laboratory block.
⑪ Power house.

Inspection monorail: Tracy Island's main underground facilities are all connected by the internal monorail system.

SYSTEMS DATA

From the lounge, the three main hangars can be reached by dedicated crew access systems, or via interlinked tunnels and elevators. For internal transport between each hangar and other subterranean sections of the island, a monorail has also been installed, which by means of a recently added spur link connects Tracy Island with neighbouring Mateo Island. Further transportation of materials and supplies is provided by a fleet of service vehicles powered by rechargeable atomic batteries.

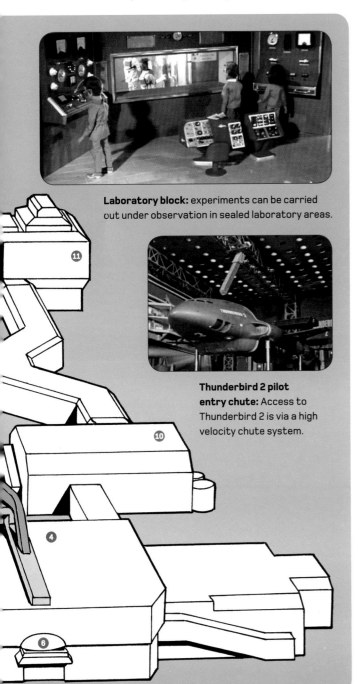

Laboratory block: experiments can be carried out under observation in sealed laboratory areas.

Thunderbird 2 pilot entry chute: Access to Thunderbird 2 is via a high velocity chute system.

Designer and Scientific Advisor
Brains

AREA OF SPECIALISATION

Conception and development of rescue craft and equipment. Mission technical support.

BACKGROUND

His real name remaining a mystery to all except his closest friends and colleagues, 'Brains' was adopted at the age of twelve by a Cambridge professor after a hurricane hit his Michigan home and left him orphaned. Recognising the young teenager's incredible scientific prowess, his surrogate father gave him every opportunity to develop his mental abilities. By the age of eighteen 'Brains' was astounding fellow scientists with his remarkable knowledge of advanced theoretical design applications during a series of lectures, following one of which he first met Jeff Tracy.

PERSONAL CHARACTERISTICS

Although he might appear absent-minded and forgetful, Brains is an intense and highly focused individual. Despite his diffident and stammering manner, he is also an accomplished marksman and an expert scuba-diver.

TRACY VILLA

Cloaked by the exterior of the Tracy Villa, Thunderbird 1 is stationed on a mobile cradle in the hangar. The pilot's cabin can be accessed immediately by its pilot via a moving platform concealed by a revolving panel in the lounge. Pilot and passenger transportation systems for Thunderbirds 2 and 3 are also built into the surrounding structure, providing direct flight-deck access.

Tracy Villa

1. Jeff Tracy's desk, from which all rescue operations are controlled.
2. Video communication screens, disguised as family portraits during 'Operation Cover-up' when visitors are present.
3. Folded into the lounge ceiling, the I.R. Agents' map can be lowered to show Jeff where operatives are located.
4. Disguised revolving door in the lounge gives Scott access to Thunderbird 1 in the adjacent hangar. Once through the door, he takes a few steps downwards and on to the retractable gantry leading to Thunderbird 1's cabin.
5. Disguised tilting wall allows Virgil to slide down the entry chute to Thunderbird 2 in its hangar.
6. Couch lift leading to Thunderbird 3's launch bay.
7. Couch repositioning arm: another couch is required to fill the hole in the lounge floor when access to Thunderbird 3 is required. As the two couches pass each other in the access shaft, the replacement is lifted from its telescopic support and moved sideways then up into the floorspace vacated by the original.
8. Thunderbird 1's soundproof hangar.
9. Retractable access gantry to Thunderbird 1. Once aboard, the gantry retracts allowing the craft to move down under the house to its launch bay.
10. Once Scott has changed into his uniform and the gantry has retracted, Thunderbird 1 can proceed down the tunnel to the launch bay.
11. Thunderbird 1 launch trolley.

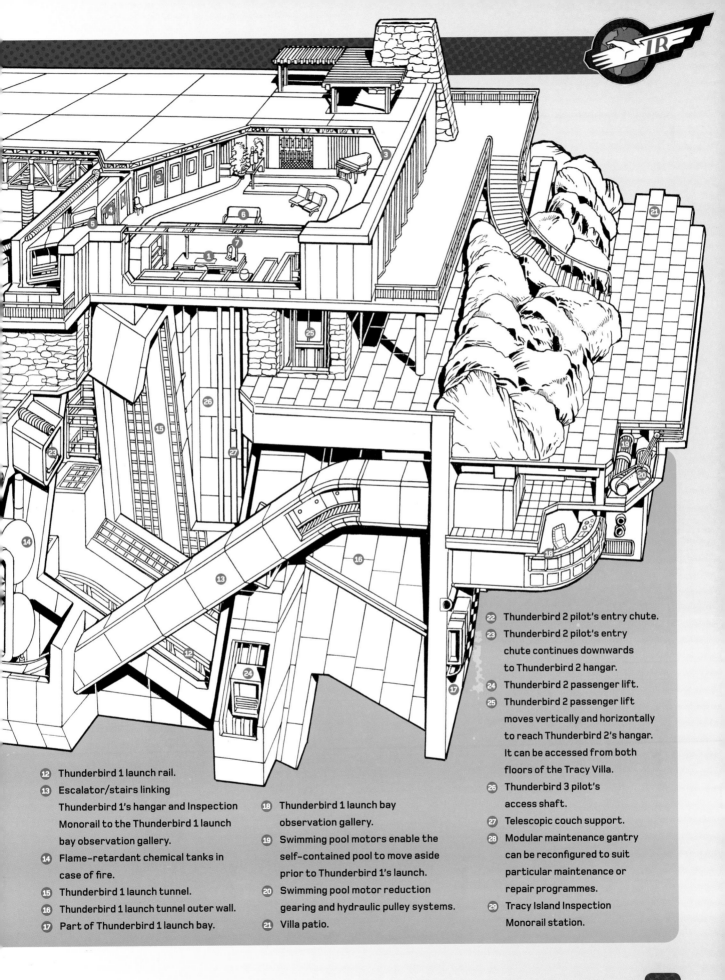

12 Thunderbird 1 launch rail.

13 Escalator/stairs linking Thunderbird 1's hangar and Inspection Monorail to the Thunderbird 1 launch bay observation gallery.

14 Flame-retardant chemical tanks in case of fire.

15 Thunderbird 1 launch tunnel.

16 Thunderbird 1 launch tunnel outer wall.

17 Part of Thunderbird 1 launch bay.

18 Thunderbird 1 launch bay observation gallery.

19 Swimming pool motors enable the self-contained pool to move aside prior to Thunderbird 1's launch.

20 Swimming pool motor reduction gearing and hydraulic pulley systems.

21 Villa patio.

22 Thunderbird 2 pilot's entry chute.

23 Thunderbird 2 pilot's entry chute continues downwards to Thunderbird 2 hangar.

24 Thunderbird 2 passenger lift.

25 Thunderbird 2 passenger lift moves vertically and horizontally to reach Thunderbird 2's hangar. It can be accessed from both floors of the Tracy Villa.

26 Thunderbird 3 pilot's access shaft.

27 Telescopic couch support.

28 Modular maintenance gantry can be reconfigured to suit particular maintenance or repair programmes.

29 Tracy Island Inspection Monorail station.

THUNDERBIRD 1 LAUNCH BAY

O nce in position directly beneath the launch aperture revealed by the sliding swimming pool, Thunderbird 1 is ready for take-off.

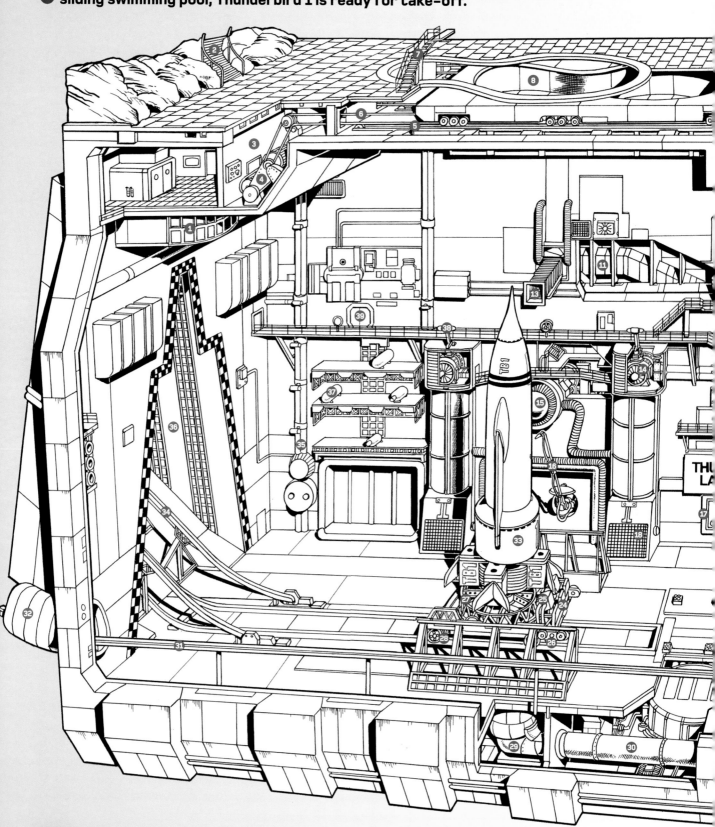

 # TB1 launch bay

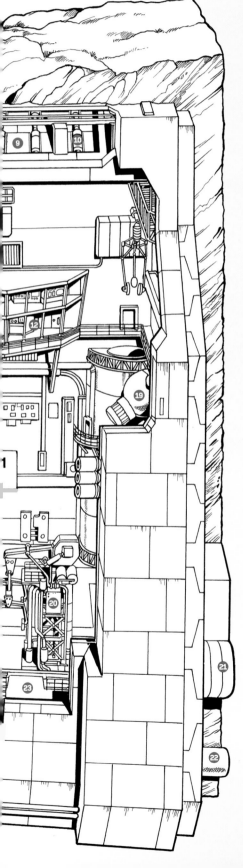

1. Observation gallery and emergency control room.
2. Steps leading to Tracy Villa first floor.
3. Swimming pool motor room.
4. Pool electric motors.
5. Pool basin support rails.
6. Pool drive belts.
7. Diving board.
8. Swimming pool water basin.
9. Pool basin holding bay, used only when Thunderbird 1 leaves, or returns to, the launch bay.
10. Pool retraction assist rollers.
11. Corridor linking the Tracy Villa to the launch bay computer galleries.
12. Launch bay computer galleries are constructed from cahelium-bonded sound- and blast-proof glass. They house the launch sequence control computers, which supply all preflight information including weather conditions over the launch area.
13. Abort gangway: in the event of an accident, the armoured door swings down and a retractable gangway can slide towards Thunderbird 1's access hatch.
14. Exhaust fume extractor fan.
15. Blower fan replaces extracted foul air with fresh air.
16. Extended fuel injection arm.
17. Air-conditioning vent.
18. Fume extraction vent duct, leading to hidden vents on the island surface.
19. High-pressure multi-nozzle foam cannon.
20. Repair/maintenance crane used if Thunderbird 1 is unable to be moved up into storage hangar.
21. Inspection Monorail tunnel leading to power plant and laboratory block.

22. Blast duct leading to filtered outlet on other side of island.
23. Thunderbird 1 launch bay Monorail access station.
24. Trolley stabilization ramps.
25. Trolley movement control computers, served by armoured blast-proof cable ducting.
26. Jockey wheels.
27. Turntable launch ring and central flame duct.
28. Trolley brake, reduction gears and motor assembly housing.
29. Blast pit.
30. Blast duct.
31. Inspection Monorail.
32. Inspection Monorail tunnel leading to the Tracy Villa and Thunderbird 1 storage hangar.
33. Thunderbird 1 on its turntable launch ring. Although it can be launched from any upright position, Thunderbird 1 is often rotated 90 degrees to that access hatch faces the abort gangway on the adjacent wall. The rotation and adjustment can take place in the tunnel or in the launch bay itself.
34. Load-bearing guide rails on which the trolley's forward wheels and safety jockey wheels run. Jockey wheels ensure Thunderbird 1 doesn't topple if the trolley ramps fail to keep the rocket platform level.
35. Air-conditioning conduits.
36. Tunnel connecting Thunderbird 1 storage hangar to launch bay.
37. Flame-retardant chemical tanks.
38. One of four beam guidance sensors (only two shown) ensure that Thunderbird 1 lands squarely on the launch trolley when returning to the launch bay after a mission.
39. Maintenance access door.

THUNDERBIRD 2 HANGAR

Concealed behind a retractable rock face door, Thunderbird 2 stands ready for launch in its hangar awaiting selection of a mission pod. Once the required pod is positioned beneath the craft and adjacent pods have been repositioned by conveyor belt, Thunderbird 2 is lowered over the container section before moving out of the launch bay.

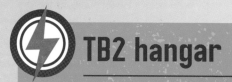

TB2 hangar

1. Dual-purpose Thunderbird 2 passenger lift cage. On rescue missions it is lowered into Thunderbird 2 with additional personnel seconds after Virgil's arrival. It can also continue onwards providing access to the Cliff House.
2. Thunderbird 2 hangar Monorail access station.
3. Inspection Monorail.
4. Retractable pilot's entry chute.
5. Thunderbird 2 pilot's launch chute linking the Tracy Villa to Thunderbird 2's flight deck.
6. Passenger lift tunnel linking the Tracy Villa with Thunderbird 2 or the Cliff House.
7. Partly retracted telescopic passenger lift chute lowers additional personnel to Thunderbird 2's flight deck.
8. Sound- and blast-proof hangar control room used for Thunderbird 2 maintenance, equipment selection and upgrade testing.
9. Manual pod selection control console.

10. Fuel line.
11. Thunderbird 2 jet engine fuel injection booms.
12. Heavily protected jet fuel storage used for Thunderbird 2's non-atomic propulsion systems and other aircraft.
13. Armoured fuel tank maintenance doors.
14. Lift shaft lowers passenger lift cage down to the Cliff House if it isn't required to deliver personnel to Thunderbird 2.
15. Hangar ventilation ducts.
16. Access to passenger lift.
17. Cliff House emergency control room, used if the Villa's control systems are compromised, or if there are problems with Thunderbird 2.
18. Power plant reservoir and pump complex serving the door hydraulic systems.
19. Steel-backed rock face door.
20. Hangar drawbridge swings down providing smooth access to the runway when the Cliff door is lowered.
21. Mobile repair and maintenance gantries

22. Access tunnel linking gallery workshops, storerooms and Cliff House with launch bay ground floor.
23. Corridor linking gallery levels to Cliff House, ground floor and pod bays. The corridors and tunnels are wide enough to allow small vehicles to be used when ferrying parts or supplies around the base.
24. Hangar ventilation and foul air extraction systems.
25. Access tunnel to laboratory block, workshops and power house.

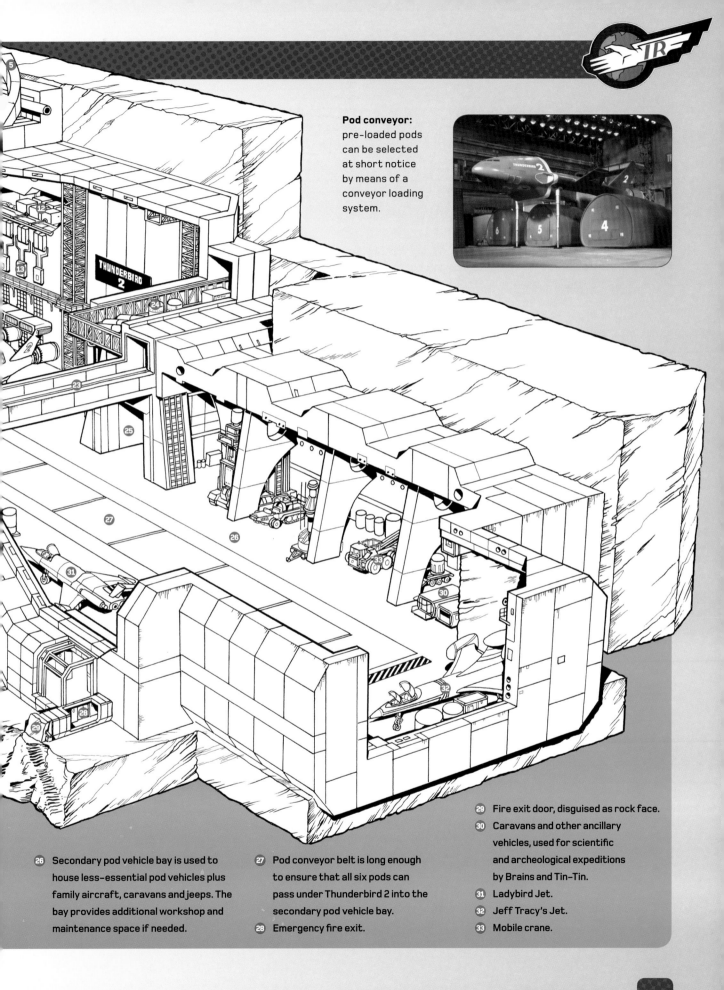

Pod conveyor: pre-loaded pods can be selected at short notice by means of a conveyor loading system.

26 Secondary pod vehicle bay is used to house less-essential pod vehicles plus family aircraft, caravans and jeeps. The bay provides additional workshop and maintenance space if needed.

27 Pod conveyor belt is long enough to ensure that all six pods can pass under Thunderbird 2 into the secondary pod vehicle bay.

28 Emergency fire exit.

29 Fire exit door, disguised as rock face.

30 Caravans and other ancillary vehicles, used for scientific and archeological expeditions by Brains and Tin-Tin.

31 Ladybird Jet.

32 Jeff Tracy's Jet.

33 Mobile crane.

THUNDERBIRD 2 POD BAY

Storage and maintenance area for ancillary rescue vehicles and pod containers. A computer-managed automated system enables pods to be loaded with unmanned vehicles operated by remote control depending on computer or human decision based analysis of potential rescue requirements.

 TB2 pod bay

1. Pod conveyor comprises one super-strength belt, the top layer of which is divided into six smaller conveyors – effectively one for each pod. This enables the pods to be moved sideways individually providing additional space between them for maintenance. Once a pod has been selected for a mission, its neighbours can be moved outwards either side of Thunderbird 2 to prevent wing damage to the craft before launch.

2. Once of six individual conveyors.

3. Individual conveyor secondary rollers.

4. Main conveyor.

5. Main conveyor rollers.

6. Individual conveyor roller sub-system.

7. Area at end of pod conveyor allows vehicles to be driven around to and from the front of each pod as required.

8. Conveyor-based pod maintenance gantries

9. Lighting rig.

10. Four of the pods have a door at the rear, which is used occasionally to load vehicles prior to a mission but rarely used during rescue operations themselves.

11. Large internal area allows vehicles to be driven in and around the pods if rescue missions require specific pod vehicle combinations.

12. Launch bay control galleries.

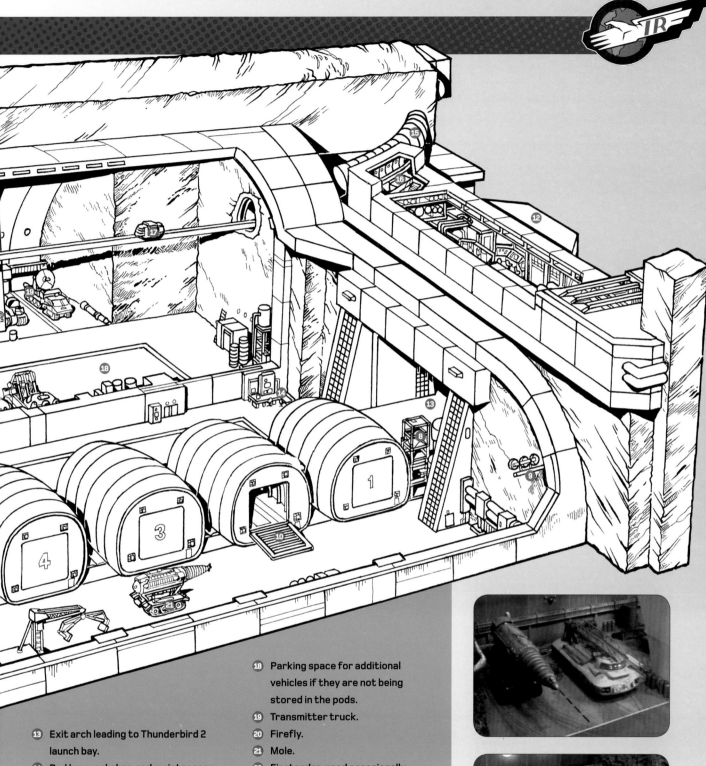

13 Exit arch leading to Thunderbird 2 launch bay.

14 Pod bay workshop and maintenance equipment.

15 Monorail tunnel continues to power plant via underground laboratories.

16 Inspection Monorail station allows access to Thunderbird 2 launch bay and pod vehicle storage bay.

17 Inspection Monorail.

18 Parking space for additional vehicles if they are not being stored in the pods.

19 Transmitter truck.

20 Firefly.

21 Mole.

22 Firetender, used occasionally as a backup to the Firefly.

23 Vehicle bay workshop and maintenance equipment.

24 Firedoor connecting pod vehicle storage bay to pod conveyor area.

25 Fuel tanks.

26 Monorail tunnel continues to Thunderbird 3 launch bay.

Storage bay: servicing and upgrades can be carried out on pod vehicles in this area.

THUNDERBIRD 2 LAUNCH RAMP

To facilitate Thunderbird 2's launch procedure, concealed hydraulics incorporated into the artificial palm trees lining the runway are operated to lower them into a tilted position preventing obstruction of Thunderbird 2's wingspan. On reaching its concealed launch ramp and exhaust extractor, the craft fires its rear thrusters to become airborne. The projecting seaward end of the runway can also be lowered to provide a ramp for Thunderbird 4 if hover-powered launch mode is selected.

Thunderbird 2 launch: the use of a concealed ramp allows Thunderbird 2 to be launched with maximum efficiency, cutting mission response time.

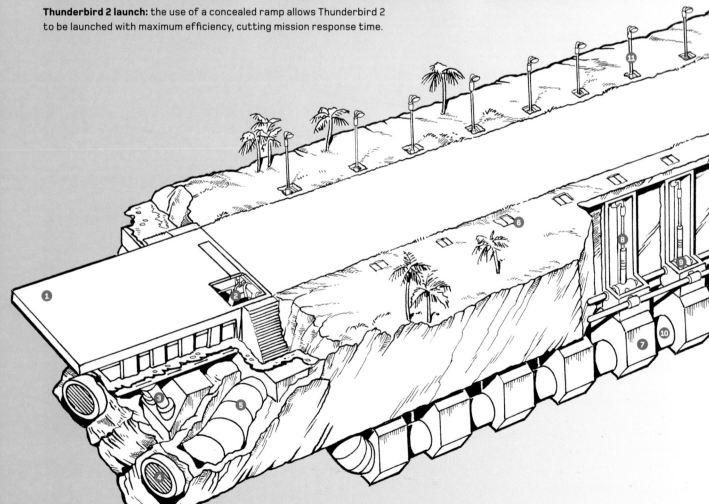

TB2 launch ramp

1. Runway pier extension doubles as a landing stage for small boats up to the size of FAB 2.

2. Runway pier hydraulics enable the end of the pier to lower into the water if Thunderbird 4 is launched without being carried in Thunderbird 2.

3. Pier hydraulic support stanchion.

4. Blast duct outlet shutters open automatically when Thunderbird 2 takes off, remaining closed at all other times.

5. Blast duct rises above sea level beneath the runway before turning downwards beneath the pier to prevent flooding.

6. Water/foam cannon access hatches.

7. Blast duct support structure.

8. Retracted water/foam cannon.

9. Foam chemical filter incorporating bypass ducts and valves enabling precision control of cannon on different sections of the runway.

10. One of two blast ducts leading to underwater outlets beneath the runway pier extension at the water's edge.

11. Water/foam cannon shown in deployed position.

12. Thunderbird 2 ramp hydraulic rams.

13. Thunderbird 2 launch ramp.

14. Heavy-duty Thunderbird 2 ramp hydraulics electric motor.

15. Blast shield forces Thunderbird 2's rear exhaust into twin blast ducts on take-off.

16. Blast pit.

17. Water cannon silo drainage pipe.

18. Water cannon silos.

19. High-pressure water/foam cannon supply pipe.

20. High-pressure turbine provides power for runway water/foam cannon.

21. Low-pressure water pipe provides nutrients and fresh water to ensure the moving palm trees are maintained in a healthy condition.

22. Nutrient container hydraulic rams.

23. Palm trees planted in nutrient containers swing outwards when Thunderbird 2 is launched.

24. Water pipes from the island's water filtration and purification plant.

25. Cliff House door provides access for Thunderbird 4 to launch if Thunderbird 2 is out of action or not required.

26. Cliff House and emergency control room.

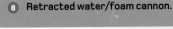

By means of a non-flexing hydraulic ram, Thunderbird 3's launch couch is lowered onto a rail-mounted automated flat-bed transporter, which carries its occupants through a link tunnel to the launch silo of Thunderbird 3.

Couch transporter: as Thunderbird 3's launch silo is some distance from the main house, a rapid transit rail link transports the launch couch through an underground tunnel.

TB3 couch transit

1. Tracy Villa lounge, where couch is normally positioned.
2. Thunderbird 3 pilot's launch couch.
3. Hydraulic lift placed directly beneath the Thunderbird 3 launch couch carries it down from the lounge to the motorized trolley at the bottom of the shaft.
4. Secondary hydraulic lift carries the replacement couch up through the Tracy Villa to the original's position in the lounge.
5. Replacement couch is lifted from top of hydraulic lift and positioned directly above the couch carrying Thunderbird 3's pilot to the launch silo.
6. Motorized trolley takes Thunderbird 3 pilot and crew to and from launch silo once sofa has locked into position.

7. Once the lift has retracted, the railway carries the couch on its trolley to the launch silo.
8. Part of the Tracy Villa.
9. Replacement couch hydraulic lift.
10. Replacement couch position arms.
11. Part of Thunderbird 2 pilot's launch chute.
12. Emergency stairwell to lift shaft floor.
13. Tunnel leading to Thunderbird 3 launch silo.
14. Lift motors.
15. Part of the access tunnel linking Thunderbird 1's hangar with Thunderbird 1's launch bay observation gallery.
16. Thunderbird 2 passenger lift shaft descends past Thunderbird 1's launch tunnel on its way down to Thunderbird 2's launch bay.

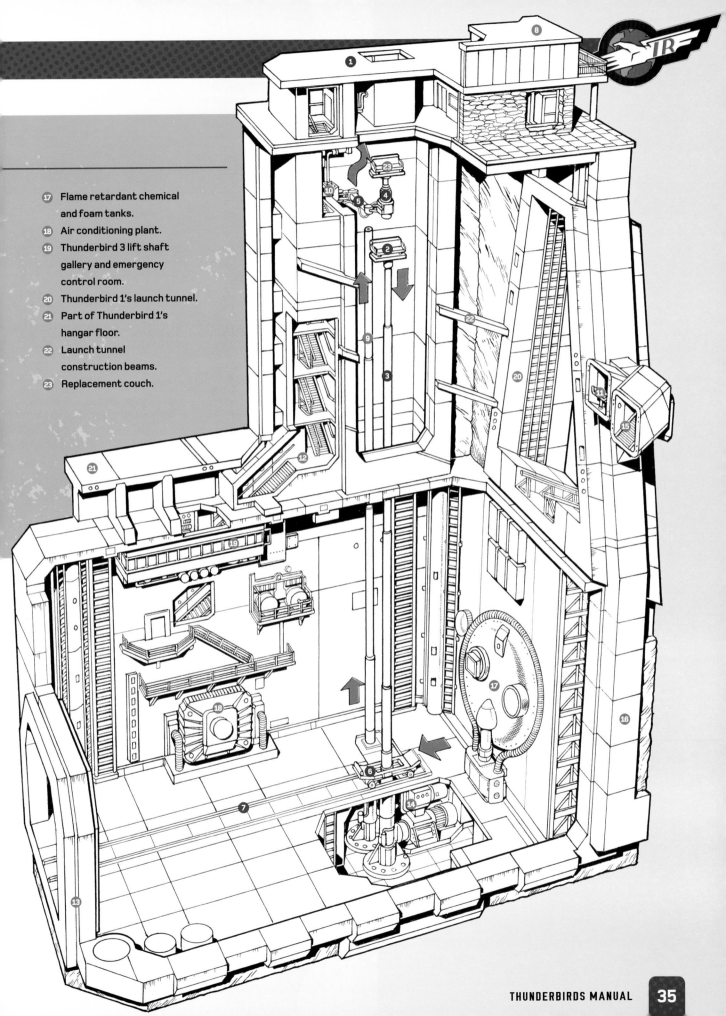

17 Flame retardant chemical and foam tanks.

18 Air conditioning plant.

19 Thunderbird 3 lift shaft gallery and emergency control room.

20 Thunderbird 1's launch tunnel.

21 Part of Thunderbird 1's hangar floor.

22 Launch tunnel construction beams.

23 Replacement couch.

When in position beneath Thunderbird 3's main fuselage, the launch couch is raised into the base of the craft and elevated through the ship to the control cabin. Once pre-launch checks have been carried out, Thunderbird 3 blasts off through the centre of the Round House.

The Round House: visitors to Tracy Island would never suspect that the area beneath the Round House conceals a three hundred foot space rocket.

TB3 launch silo

1. Forcefield and sensor array built into the inner heat resistant wall ensures Thunderbird 3 doesn't collide with the Round House when lifting off or returning to base.
2. Round House primary support columns.
3. Solar panels.
4. Three storey Round House comprises two levels of bedrooms and living areas, plus one lower level for utilities, including laundry rooms and storage areas.
5. Steps to lower floor of Round House.
6. Thunderbird 3 silo door. Although often left open, the launch bay silo door can be closed if the Round House has visitors. It is disguised as a central patio.
7. An additional column under the entrance steps provides extra support to the Round House structure.
8. Video camera and guidance sensor ensures Thunderbird 3 lands squarely as the support columns at the base of the silo.

9. Silo door slot and operating system.
10. Silo roof lighting.
11. Clean air ventilation fans.
12. Air ventilation duct.
13. Foul air dispersion pipes, leading to vents immediately below the Round House silo doors.
14. Exhaust and foul air extraction turbines built into silo walls.
15. Foul air/exhaust extraction vents.
16. Booster rocket fuel injection systems.
17. Fuel lines for Thunderbird 3's booster rockets.
18. Retracted maintenance crane.
19. Nuclear fusion generator powers all silo maintenance and ventilation systems.
20. Electricity generators.
21. Blast ducts leading to outlets below sea level.
22. Blast duct cooling water injection nozzles.
23. Thrust absorbtion bracing struts.
24. Shock absorbers.
25. Support column water cooling pumps.
26. Blast extraction turbofan.
27. Exhaust blast duct.

28. Launch trolley on which the sofa is conveyed to Thunderbird 3.
29. Hydraulic ram lifts sofa up into Thunderbird 3.
30. Launch trolley railway line leading to lift silo beneath the Tracy Villa.
31. Inspection monorail.
32. Footpath passageway links station to silo.
33. Steps to ground level built into silo wall.
34. Exit to monorail.
35. Monorail support column.
36. Monorail station provides access via footpath passageway to launch silo.
37. Monorail tunnel leading to Thunderbird 2 launch bay and pod vehicle storage areas.
38. Monorail tunnel leading to the Tracy Villa and Thunderbird 1's hangar via the underground boat pen.
39. Monorail points assembly disengages track to allow the inspection car to change course.
40. Fuel lines for booster rockets leading to fuel store adjacent to the power house.

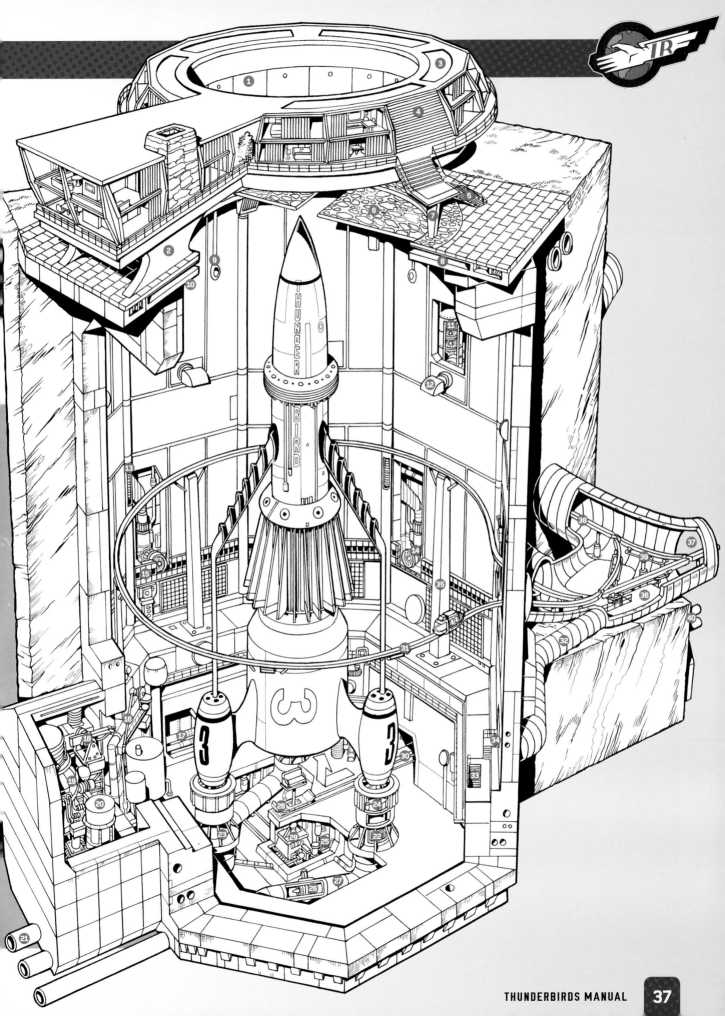

ADDITIONAL FACILITIES

In addition to the main hangars, other naturally formed caverns beneath Tracy Island have been adapted to house a compact power plant and a complex of laboratories and construction bays enabling Brains to carry out research and experimental development to create new rescue devices and vehicles.

Experimental facilities: new equipment can be tested under controlled conditions in these underground areas.

Additional facilities

1. Monorail station accessing the laboratory complex.
2. Monorail tunnel.
3. Waste and sewerage pipe leading to treatment plant.
4. Blast duct from Thunderbird 1's launch bay.
5. Reactor and turbine maintenance control block.
6. Emergency use only tunnel station.
7. Power plant emergency shelter blockhouse.
8. Power conduits connecting the power plant to the islands' underground installations.
9. Monorail tunnel leading to Thunderbird 1 launch bay.

10. Powerhouse monorail station.
11. Fuel pipes leading to Thunderbird 1's launch bay.
12. Thunderbird 1's fuel storage tanks.
13. Shielded powerhouse.
14. Primary turbine, powered by adjacent fusion reactor.
15. Heat exchanger.
16. Atomic fusion reactor.
17. Powerhouse roof: the reactor was originally installed into the powerhouse from above; the shielded roof was built over the top and then buried under topsoil.
18. Reactor and power plant construction cranes originally used to install the reactor are now used for maintenance duties.
19. Brains's main laboratory: although there is a laboratory in the Tracy Villa, the underground complex is better equipped to create and maintain Brains's larger projects and inventions.

20. Pod vehicle maintenance and construction gantry. If major maintenance, repair or upgrading work is required, pod vehicles can be brought into the laboratory block, giving Brains easy access to them from his adjacent laboratory.
21. Extra-wide heavy-duty tunnel connects Thunderbird 2's hangar to the power plant via the laboratory complex. The tunnel zig-zags to minimise the incline and is used for power plant maintenance and fuel deliveries.
22. Seawater filteration and purification plant.
23. Laboratory blockhouse.
24. Tunnel leading to Thunderbird 2 launch bay.
25. Heavy-duty cranes.
26. Inspection monorail leading to Thunderbird 2 launch bay and pod vehicle storage bays.

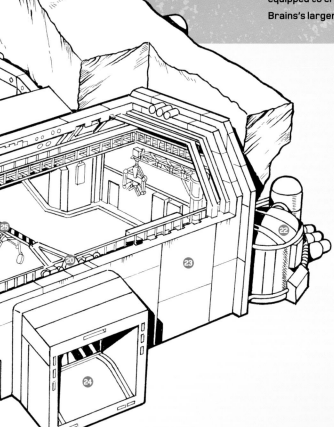

Laboratories: Brains has been provided with a number of laboratories, equipped with the latest scientific devices.

MATEO ISLAND

In the event of emergencies and to provide additional service facilities, nearby Mateo Island has also been converted for International Rescue's use by the Tracy family. A monorail link to the main island allows access and transportation of supplies without drawing attention to the organisation's activities

Overview

1. Graphite and concrete re-inforced power house block.
2. Atomic fusion reactor.
3. Air recycling and pumping station.
4. Access passage leading to powerhouse, air pumping station and communications station.
5. Air circulation pipes are used in conjunction with – and separately if necessary – access passages to provide ventilation throughout the islands' installations.
6. Deployed emergency satellite communications station.
7. Rock-face disguised communications antennae doors.
8. Rock-face disguised hangar doors, shown in opened positions.
9. Hydraulic supports raise and lower the disguised hangar doors. When closed, only the closest of inspections would reveal an entrance to the emergency launch bay for Thunderbird 3.
10. Thunderbird 3 emergency launch bay. Used if the main launch bay on Tracy Island is out of action or being upgraded.
11. Thunderbird 3 rocket nacelle support columns. Blast ducts lead to submerged outlets on other side of island.
12. Telescopic support column of the topside hangar landing tower column incorporates fuel feed lines leading via the adjacent pump to the fuel tank chamber.
13. Passage to Thunderbird 3 hangar.
14. Rock-face disguised hangar doors to the topside hangar, shown partly opened.
15. Tracy family jet.
16. Small aircraft fuel pump.
17. Fuel tank chamber concrete blast shield.
18. Cahelium-strengthened fuel tanks, linked via undersea pipeline to Tracy Island.
19. Fuel feed/distribution pumps.
20. Fuel retrieval pump system in deployed position. Can be operated by the crew of the supply tanker without the need of the Tracy family to be present during fuel collection operations.
21. Fuel retrieval pump positioning conveyor.
22. Disguised rockface 'up and over' doors.
23. Forward electro-magnetic clamp.
24. Water pump inlets.
25. Fuel pipe linking cliff terminal to fuel tanks.
26. Water pump turbines used to flood fuel tank chamber in the event of a fire.
27. Auto-fuel feed pumps.
28. Telescopic fuel injection arms.
29. Auto-repair and maintenance gantries, normally concealed behind interior rock face doors of the main hangar.

30 Maintenance gantry disguised rockface door.

31 Fire exit.

32 Disguised rock face door shown in lowered position.

33 Aircraft turning area, accessed from disguised door in main hangar.

34 Repair, servicing and storage bay.

35 Main hangar lighting.

36 Main hangar: although sealed from the outside world, the hangar is disguised to look like a roughly-hollowed out natural cave with a minimum of support systems on view.

37 Disguised rock–cliff door slides downwards to reveal entrance to main hangar.

38 Docking bay for small family boats and, if required, Thunderbird 4.

39 Sea level disguised door allows Thunderbird 4 or other craft to access the docking bay.

40 Access passages linking Thunderbird 4 bay to main hangar.

THUNDERBIRD 1

International Rescue's high speed reconnaissance craft, Thunderbird 1 is designed for maximum speed and operational flexibility.

Thunderbird 1
Technical data

DIMENSIONS
LENGTH: 115 feet
WINGSPAN: 80 feet
DIAMETER: 12 feet
WEIGHT: 140 tons

PERFORMANCE
MAX SPEED: 15,000mph
MAX ALTITUDE: 150,000 feet
RANGE: Unlimited

POWER
POWER SOURCE: Atomic fusion reactor
ENGINES: 4 variable-cycle gas turbine engines; 4 booster rockets; 1 variable-mode engine operating as a high-performance sustainer rocket for launch or boost or as a variable-cycle gas turbine engine in flight; 1 vertical take-off variable-mode engine operating as a rocket or variable-cycle gas turbine hover jet

TECHNOLOGY DATA FILE

An innovative combination of standard rocket-ship and swing-wing fighter plane, Thunderbird 1 is powered by conventionally fuelled rockets and a molten metal atomic fusion reactor. A centrally mounted variable mode thruster operates as a high-performance sustainer rocket for launch and emergency boost, and in gas-turbine mode during flight. Four additional booster rockets mounted on the tail unit supply extra power for launch and are flanked by four ramjet turbines that provide directional flight control. For horizontal landing, power is transferred to a separate centrally mounted VTOL rocket.

With sufficient power to reach a maximum speed of 15,000mph at an altitude of 150,000 feet, top-secret new technology has been developed by Brains to prevent stratospheric disintegration. This takes the form of the HALO (High Altitude Operating) system incorporating MIDAS (Molecular Interspatial Disturbance Anti-detection Shroud), and provides a distortional force field, which serves the dual function of acting as a protective barrier against external air pressure and as an effective radar-jamming cloak. The resultant capability to attain previously unthinkable speeds allows Thunderbird 1 to reach potential danger zones in the most remote parts of the world in record time, allowing its pilot every opportunity to maximise mission assessment analysis.

Control of Thunderbird 1 is maintained from a gimbal mounted pilot's seat in the nose-cone section, which incorporates navigational and multifunction subsidiary equipment operation via twist-grip side positioned levers. A forward-mounted display screen provides inflight visual information, while observation ports on either side of the cabin can be unshielded for extra visibility.

On arrival at a danger zone, Thunderbird 1 can land horizontally on any terrain with optional wheel or skid-mounted undercarriage, or hold station in mid-air with the use of a hover-jet positioning system. The craft's pilot also has a selection of devices available to facilitate rescue operations, including a mobile inspection camera, sonar sounding equipment, a winch system, high-velocity spears, a magnetic grapple and a retractable destructor cannon. A variety of field equipment, medical supplies and protective clothing is also stored in control cabin lockers.

In addition to equipment stored in the control cabin, a storage bay in the rear fuselage houses a mobile control unit and a personal hover-jet. For security purposes Thunderbird 1 is fitted with dual automatic camera detectors and a digital- and magnetic-image wiping beam. If any film images are found to have been recorded, however, other means have to be found to arrange for their physical destruction.

Pilot
Thunderbird 1
Scott Tracy

AREA OF SPECIALISATION
Danger zone mission assessment and command. Second in command of International Rescue

BACKGROUND
Educated at Yale and Oxford prior to astronaut training at Tracy College on the University of Kansas campus, and a highly decorated term of service in the U.S. Air Force, Scott was the natural choice to be given command of Thunderbird 1. His experience in handling a variety of cutting-edge fighter planes and rocket-ships has given him the ideal grounding to fly the world's most advanced high-speed aircraft.

PERSONAL CHARACTERISTICS
Quick-witted, bold and decisive, Scott has a flair for leadership and pressurised decision making. This capacity for clear thinking in extreme circumstances is of great benefit during rescue operations. Off duty, Scott is relaxed and good humoured with a love of home cooking.

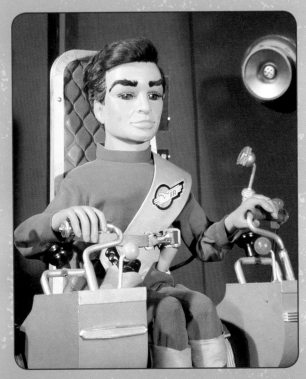

THUNDERBIRD 1

Thunderbird 1 is International Rescue's scout craft. Capable of reaching speeds of up to 15,000mph through the use of advanced aeronautical technology, it is powered by a combination of rocket fuel and atomic fusion. On arrival at a danger zone it can land horizontally or hover in mid-air as a mobile command centre.

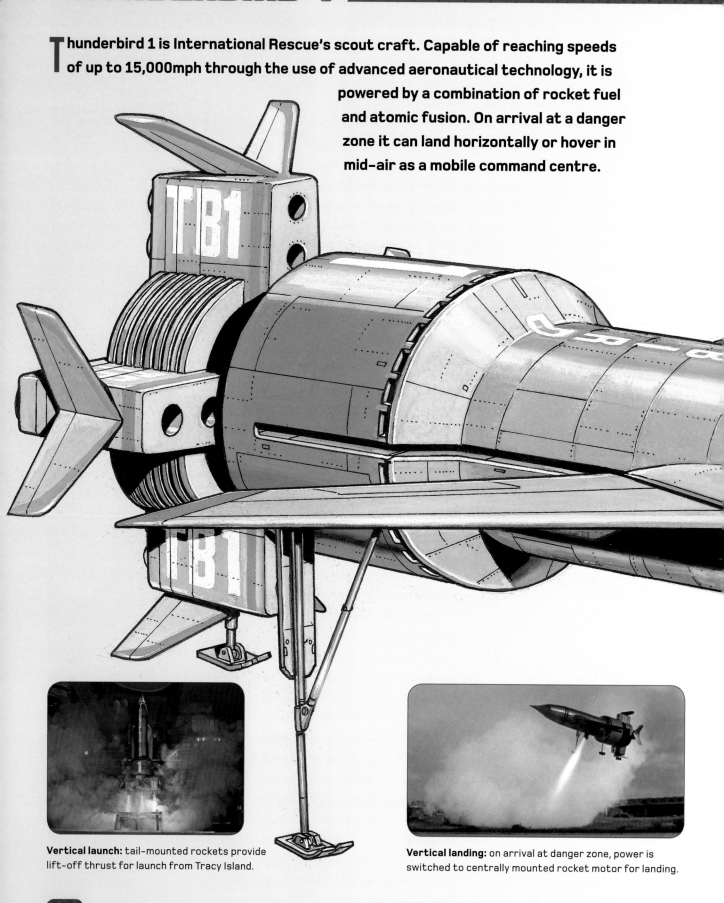

Vertical launch: tail-mounted rockets provide lift-off thrust for launch from Tracy Island.

Vertical landing: on arrival at danger zone, power is switched to centrally mounted rocket motor for landing.

TB1 Overview

1. Life-support systems and air recycling/carbon dioxide conversion unit.
2. Cabin air tanks.
3. Cockpit bulkhead.
4. Starboard-mounted Automatic Camera Detector.
5. Pilot's seat support frame.
6. Pilot's seat geared rotation gimbals.
7. Additional bucket seat attachment jacks.
8. Steering/altitude controls.
9. Engine throttle controls.
10. Pilot's seat rotates to remain upright when Thunderbird 1 changes from vertical to horizontal flight.
11. Pilot exit hatch.
12. Forward pitch and yaw jets.
13. Pitch and yaw jet nozzle outlets.
14. Console-mounted computerised instrumentation system links nose-cone radar and avionics systems to instrument panel interface. Simplified instrument panel enables fine control of aircraft at speeds up to 15,000mph.
15. Instrument panel bulkhead.
16. Neutroni Communications transmitter/receiver.
17. Radar ranging unit.
18. Radar scanner dish.
19. M.I.D.A.S. system: Molecular Interspatial Displacement Anti-detection Shroud cloaks Thunderbird 1 from military and civilian radar/satellite detection systems. Also installed in Thunderbird 2 and 3, the MIDAS system prevents the I.R. craft from being tracked in flight to and from Tracy Island.
20. MIDAS mounting frame.
21. Telemetry and Avionics inner pressure and heat protection cone.
22. Heat-resistant Cahelium-bonded nose cone.

Cannon: a destructor cannon is used to carry out demolition work or to clear hazardous areas.

Cockpit: Thunderbird 1 is flown from an enclosed cockpit with the aid of computer guidance systems.

The nerve centre of Thunderbird 1, the craft's cockpit is packed with navigational technology and emergency rescue devices. Like all International Rescue craft and equipment, Thunderbird 1 is continually being modified, and the craft's cockpit has seen a number of upgrades while in operational use.

Multi-function video display: all visual information for flight control and communication is transmitted through the control cabin video display screen.

Cockpit

1. Console-mounted computerised instrumentation system links nose-cone radar and avionics systems to console video screen and displays.
2. Telemetry and avionics inner pressure and heat protection cone.
3. Pitch and yaw jet attachment jacks.
4. Pitch and yaw jet linkage wells.
5. Jet fuel pipe outlets.

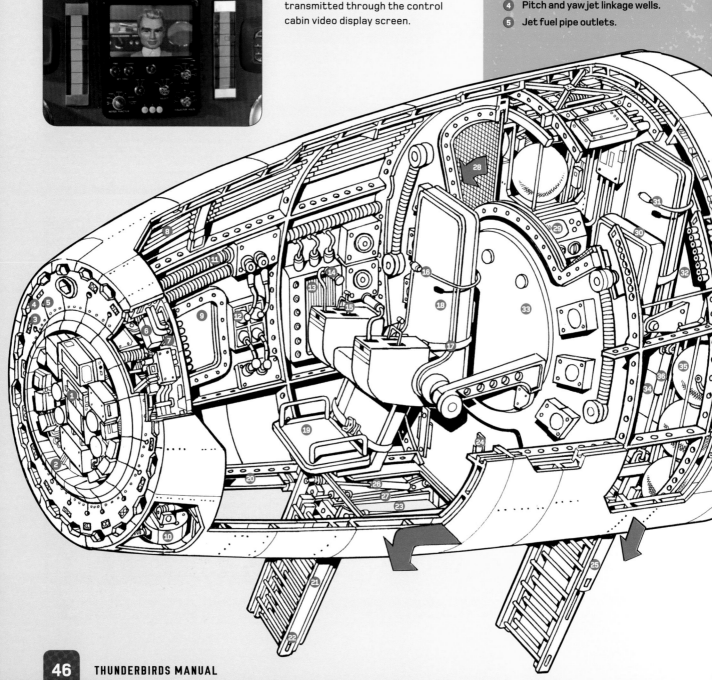

6. Control console interface transfers piloting commands from pilot seat controls and console to flight computer.
7. Fuel feed pipe distribution valves.
8. Pitch and yaw jet fuel lines.
9. Starboard observation window.
10. Retracted International Engineering Ltd TBM6 20mm swivel machine cannon.
11. Cabin pressure air ducting.
12. Life-support systems and air-recycling unit.
13. Cabin air-conditioning unit.
14. Steering/altitude controls.
15. Engine throttle controls.
16. Communications microphone
17. Safety harness.
18. Pilot's seat rotates to remain upright when Thunderbird 1 changes from vertical to horizontal flight.
19. Footrest in lowered/deployed position.
20. Cockpit access hatch door.
21. Pilot's cockpit access ladder shown in partly deployed position.
22. Automated ladder safety locks.
23. Ladder storage well.
24. Additional bucket seat attachment jacks.
25. Passenger seat access ladder shown in partly deployed position.
26. Cockpit ladder deployment hydraulics.
27. Ladder deployment slider: ladder slides forwards then downwards when needed.
28. Bulkhead screen moves around centre section of bulkhead to allow verbal communication between pilot and (optional) passenger.
29. Passenger seat computer monitor relays flight data from Thunderbird 1's control systems plus rescue mission data from Thunderbird 5 if required.
30. Passenger seat in stowed upright position. Footrest is stowed in upright position on the back of the cockpit bulkhead.
31. Passenger seat microphone enables Brains or another I.R. operative to communicate with the pilot, Tracy Island or other sources.
32. Rear pressure bulkhead.
33. Cockpit bulkhead.
34. Passenger cabin ladder storage well: when retracted, the access ladder is stored under the passenger seat.
35. Cabin air tanks.
36. Access ladder deployment hydraulics.

CONTROL SYSTEMS

Control of Thunderbird 1 is maintained by manual function selectors linked to a computerised navigational system and forward-mounted display units. The main viewing screen provides inflight information and can be switched between targeting, infrared, thermal imaging, sonar, radar, video communication and remote camera modes. To assist the pilot in danger-zone risk assessment, Thunderbird 1 is equipped with a number of survey devices including a remote temperature-resistant hover camera, sonar sounding pod and a range of environmental status sensors. If immediate action is required prior to the arrival of heavy rescue equipment, Thunderbird 1's pilot can also call on a variety of general-purpose accessories, which include a magnetic grapple connected to a winch cable, a set of Cahelium-X-tipped spears, which can provide an anti-debris screen, and a high-powered destructor cannon designed for demolition of potentially hazardous structures.

A. Flight systems computer diagnostic display.
B. External environment indicator.
C. Life-support controls.
D. Port twist-grip booster control.
E. Microphone.
F. Port viewing hatch.
G. Port VTOL thruster control.
H. Auxiliary equipment function selector.
I. Altitude meter.
J. Cabin pressure meter.
K. Air speed indicator.
L. Starboard VTOL thruster control.
M. Auxiliary equipment control joystick.
N. Starboard viewing hatch.
O. Starboard twist-grip booster control.
P. External environment indicator.
Q. Emergency survival kit.
R. Multi-function video display.
S. Systems indicator check lights.

THUNDERBIRD 1

A marvel of technological ingenuity, Thunderbird 1's retractable wings and atomic rocket propulsion systems are compactly incorporated into the craft's slim streamlined fuselage and rear-mounted booster assembly.

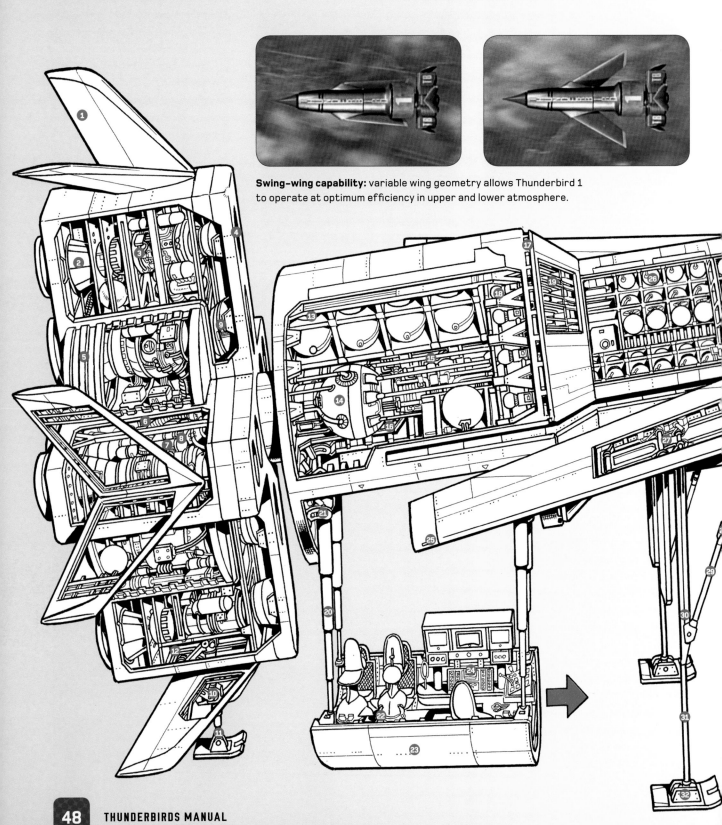

Swing-wing capability: variable wing geometry allows Thunderbird 1 to operate at optimum efficiency in upper and lower atmosphere.

Propulsion and equipment

1. Topside stabilising fin.
2. Ramjet thrust pipe.
3. Heat exchanger: molten metal circulated from reactor passes heat which exhausts at ramjet thrust pipe.
4. Ramjet air intake.
5. Turbojet cooling vanes.
6. Centrally mounted variable-mode engine operates as a sustainer rocket for take off and as a gas turbine engine in flight.

12. Landing leg inflight storage well.
13. Booster rocket primary fuel tanks.
14. Graphite and Cahelium-shielded atomic fusion reactor.
15. Reactor surface cooling pipes.

26. Turbojet fuel tanks.
27. Landing leg and hatch deployment actuators.
28. Support strut retraction hinge.
29. Landing leg support strut.
30. Upper landing leg section, incorporating support strut slide and lock groove used when leg is deployed.
31. Landing leg lower telescopic section.
32. Starboard landing pad is stored flat within the wing during flight.

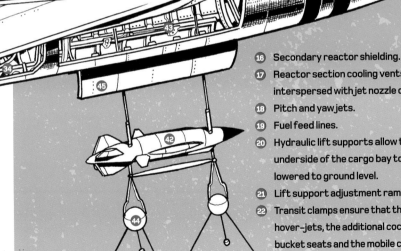

7. Turbojet heat exchanger.
8. Turbojet turbines.
9. Air intakes pass air to compressor and heat exchanger.
10. Landing leg retraction pivot.
11. Rear landing leg.

16. Secondary reactor shielding.
17. Reactor section cooling vents, interspersed with jet nozzle outlets.
18. Pitch and yaw jets.
19. Fuel feed lines.
20. Hydraulic lift supports allow the underside of the cargo bay to be lowered to ground level.
21. Lift support adjustment rams.
22. Transit clamps ensure that the two hover-jets, the additional cockpit bucket seats and the mobile control unit are undamaged and secure during TB1's varying flight configurations.
23. Reactor section lower hull doubles as a cargo deck floor for the mobile control unit, hover-jets and other equipment.
24. Mobile control unit is clamped into position during flight.
25. Wing-tip light.

33. Vertical take-off jet fuel tanks.
34. Variable-mode vertical take-off rocket and hover jet.
35. Auxiliary motors and batteries.
36. Fuselage refridgeration unit.
37. Wing carry-through box containing wing hinge.
38. Starboard wing configuration protection blister.
39. Wingroot attachment spars.
40. Hydraulic rams controlling wing retraction/deployment functions.
41. Remote control hover camera uses anti-gravity technology to enable the operator to view a disaster zone from Thunderbird 1's cabin.
42. Sonar tracking system electronics pod.
43. Sonar tracking system deployment cable drum.
44. Sonar tracking array each with three retractable antennae. The system is used to register life signs under water, and to measure depths and distances.
45. Sonar tracking bay doors.

THUNDERBIRD 2

Flagship of the International Rescue fleet, Thunderbird 2 provides the essential means of transporting specialised rescue equipment to the danger zone.

Thunderbird 2
Technical data

DIMENSIONS
LENGTH: 250 feet
WIDTH: 180 feet
HEIGHT: 60 feet
WEIGHT: 406 tons (ex. payload)
PAYLOAD: up to 100 tons

PERFORMANCE
MAXIMUM SPEED: 5,000mph
CRUISING SPEED: 2,000mph
MAXIMUM ALTITUDE: 100,000 feet
RANGE: unlimited

POWER
POWER SOURCE: Atomic fusion reactor

ENGINES: 2 variable-cycle gas turbine engines operating as turbo fans at low speed and supersonic combustion ramjets at high speed, 12 variable-cycle turbo-ram cruise/trim jets in tailplane, 4 vertical take-off fan jets in main body, 4 vertical take-off chemical rockets in landing legs

TECHNOLOGY DATA FILE

The giant workhorse of International Rescue, Thunderbird 2 was designed to meet a unique and demanding brief. A heavy-duty cargo craft was required that would be capable of transporting a range of specialist rescue vehicles ready to be selected at short notice, had the ability to travel at high speed and land in confined areas, and which would be equipped to carry out a variety of tasks on arrival at a danger zone.

The impressive solution is an inspired and versatile lifting body design utilising the ingenious idea of a fuselage that can be fitted with interchangeable pre-loaded pods to form an aerodynamically efficient wing-shaped profile. Side spars are fitted with telescopic landing legs and thrusters for vertical landing and take-off, while a two-level nose cone section houses the craft's control cabin and multi-purpose tool bay. Like its sister ship Thunderbird 2 is powered by a combination of atomic energy and conventional fuel-burning rockets.

The innovative design was only made possible due to the incorporation of the super-light and incredibly strong properties of Cahelium, which have been employed to form a bonded twin-boom support frame around which the aircraft body has been built. Only through the inherent strength of this core structure could the interchangeable pod units be integrated into the surrounding airframe.

The strength of the support frame also allows a larger version of the molten metal atomic fusion reactor fitted to Thunderbird 1 to be installed in the rear section of Thunderbird 2 to supply power to the spar-mounted thrusters and the craft's turbo-electric generators. Cruising speed is also boosted by four ramjets mounted in the rear tailplane assembly, while VTOL manoeuvrability and landing and take-off functions are powered by conventionally fuelled rocket thrusters built into the telescopic leg mechanisms. Shut off valves at the base of each landing leg transfer exhaust energy into the legs to raise the main body of the craft above the pod to allow access for the vehicles contained inside.

Integrally connected to the main support frame is a forward extension around which the split level nose cone of the craft is built. This section of Thunderbird 2 is packed with a comprehensive range of rescue equipment and supplies. The upper level comprises a control cabin, medical section, an astrodome missile targeting unit and an air-to-air rescue system. The lower deck is constructed around a central hatch through which a variety of devices can be lowered, including magnetic grabs, debris-clearance claws and a personal escape capsule. In the prow of the craft are the essential telemetry control processors, radome and detection equipment, in addition to the HALO system and MIDAS units. Combined with a revolutionary cooling unit, these enable Thunderbird 2 to reach speeds in excess of 5,000mph.

Pilot
Thunderbird 2
Virgil Tracy

AREA OF SPECIALISATION
Responsible for transportation and operation of heavy rescue equipment required for rescue missions.

BACKGROUND
In common with his father Virgil showed an early aptitude for handling the complex machinery employed on the family wheat farm. Graduating from Denver School of Advanced Technology with high-grade diplomas in mechanics and practical science, Virgil also went on to the astronaut training course at Tracy College. His intuitive mechanical dexterity ideally qualified him to pilot the heavyweight Thunderbird 2 and the various specialised vehicles deployed during rescues.

PERSONAL CHARACTERISTICS
Virgil's lightness of touch with machinery is reflected in his artistic abilities. A talented abstract painter and pianist, he has inherited his mother's love of music and art.

THUNDERBIRD 2

Thunderbird 2 provides vital heavy rescue versatility.

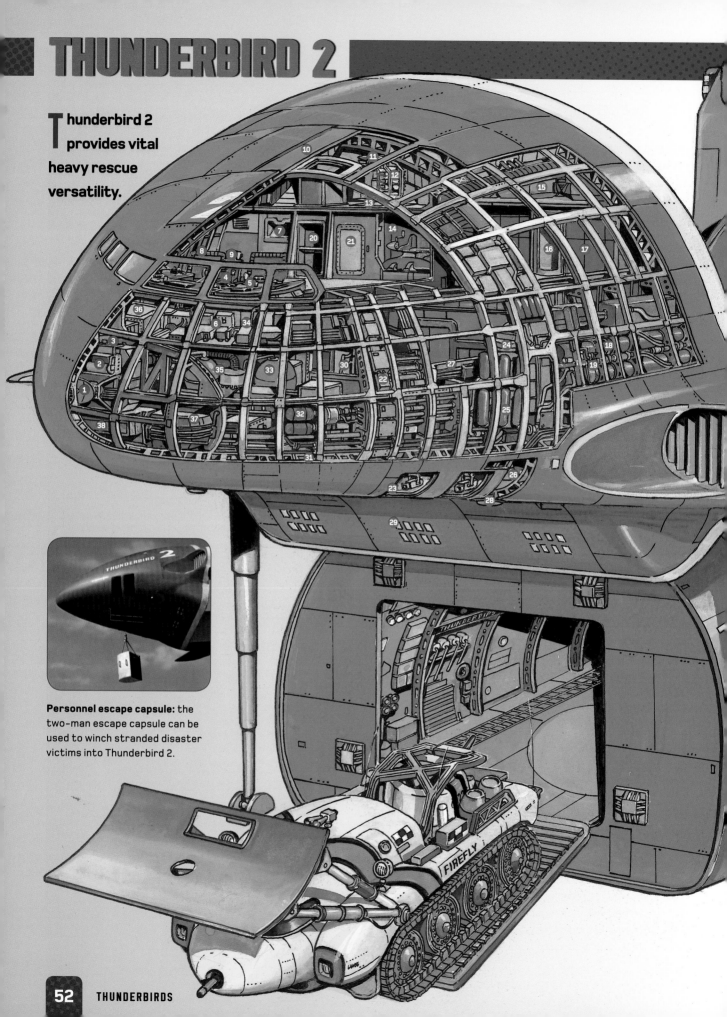

Personnel escape capsule: the two-man escape capsule can be used to winch stranded disaster victims into Thunderbird 2.

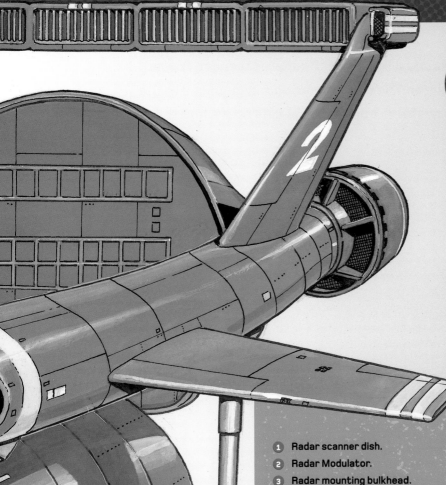

Overview

19 Fuel feed management systems.

20 Passenger lift entry point to flight deck.

21 Access hatch to hover-jet holding bay, storage lockers for rescue and medical supplies, crew accommodation and the rear access door leading to the pod inspection gallery.

22 Environment sensor control electronics.

23 Cahelium and ceramic-toughened glass observation ports with video cameras.

24 Ramjet support frame.

25 Port vertical take-off ramjet.

26 Ramjet afterburner nozzle.

27 Rescue equipment bay/engine bulkhead.

28 Nozzle outlet tube.

29 External environment sensors.

30 Forward rescue equipment bay holds a rescue cage, hawser cable launchers, electromagnetic grabs etc (see separate illustration).

31 Cooling ducts.

32 Hull cooling systems.

33 Compressed air tanks.

34 Forward pressure bulkhead.

35 Life-support systems and air recycling unit.

36 Telemetry computer transfers piloting commands from the simplified flight instrument panel to the aircraft's sophisticated control systems.

37 M.I.D.A.S. Molecular Interspatial Displacement Anti-Detection Shroud cloaks Thunderbird 2 from military and civilian radar/satellite detection systems to prevent it being tracked in flight to and from Tracy Island.

1 Radar scanner dish.

2 Radar Modulator.

3 Radar mounting bulkhead.

4 Pilot's steering column.

5 Ergonomically simplified flight instrument panel.

6 Avionics bay.

7 Entry chute delivery point on flight deck rear bulkhead provides direct access to pilot's instrument panel.

8 Additional personnel seating.

9 Pilot's seat.

10 Chute entry and missile firing hatch provides access for Virgil's entry chute and adjacent passenger lift.

11 Missile launcher.

12 Missile launch auto loader.

13 Hover-jet bay access hatch leading to chute entry hatch above.

14 Hover-jet holding bay.

15 Fuel tanks.

16 Lift connects flight deck to lower level and ground-level pod door.

17 Storage lockers.

18 Vertical take-off jet fuel tanks.

Air-to-air unit: inflight craft-to-craft transfers can be made with this unit to carry out onboard repairs and rescues.

Thunderbird 2 is constructed around a lightweight super-strength frame providing essential integral rigidity. The main power unit is mounted in the rear of the craft with propulsion systems built into the side spars and tailplane.

Propulsion and engines

1. Inverted air intake blister.
2. Ramjet air intake.
3. Landing leg foot protection blister.
4. Nacelle fuselage attachment joints.
5. Nacelle shock-absorbing hull support stanchion.
6. Landing leg storage nacelle, mid-mounted with ramjet air intake ducting.
7. Retracted telescopic landing leg: the lower segment contains vertical thrust rocket to aid take off and landing when the leg is in retracted position.
8. Landing leg power unit.
9. Air inlet ducting either side of landing leg storage nacelle.
10. Engine compressor face.
11. Port centre body ramjet.
12. Main wing attachment bolts.
13. Turbine frame fuselage support coupling.
14. Compressor turbine.
15. Primary heat exchanger.
16. Heat-resistant mid-mounted rear landing leg storage nacelle.
17. Reheat secondary heat exchanger.
18. Rear telescopic landing leg – deployed.
19. Nacelle cooling vents.
20. Ramjet thrust pipe.
21. Port nacelle housing ramjet thrust pipe surrounded by booster rockets, used in emergencies and also in launching from ramp.

22. Control and fuel lines connecting main body power systems to tailplane turbo ramjets.
23. Tailplane fin spar construction.
24. Tailplane air intakes.
25. Ram air jet turbine provides emergency power.
26. Variable-cycle turbo-ramjets.
27. Rocket fuel oxidant tank.
28. Rocket fuel tanks and pumps.
29. Atomic fusion generator supplies heat to jet exchangers and turboelectric generators.
30. Heat distribution conduits.
31. Reactor control circuits.
32. Cahelium and graphite atomic generator shield.
33. Reactor heat distribution and regulation valve control systems for starboard engines.

34. Cahelium-bonded twin-boom fuselage support frame.
35. High-strength pressure bulkhead separating starboard engine from fuselage support frame.

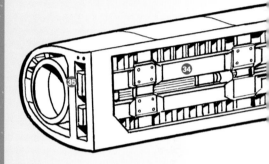

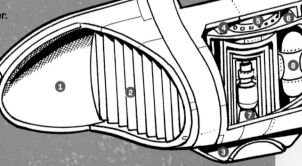

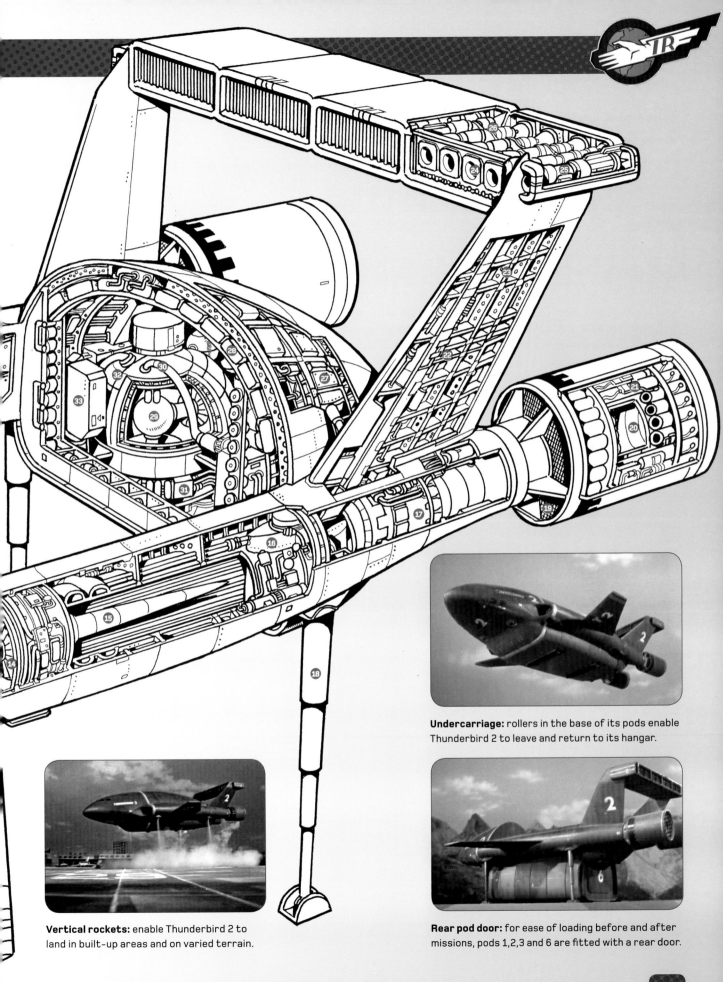

Undercarriage: rollers in the base of its pods enable Thunderbird 2 to leave and return to its hangar.

Vertical rockets: enable Thunderbird 2 to land in built-up areas and on varied terrain.

Rear pod door: for ease of loading before and after missions, pods 1,2,3 and 6 are fitted with a rear door.

The flight deck of Thunderbird 2 is situated on the upper level of the nose cone, which also incorporates missile targeting and launch systems, a medical section and air-to-air rescue equipment.

Flight deck

1. Upper storage bay.
2. Lift and adjacent access ladder to lower storage bay and equipment deck.
3. Central access corridor.
4. Bay pressurisation controls.
5. Air-to-air equipment bay hatch in open position.
6. Air-to-air equipment allows an operative to transfer from Thunderbird 2 to the underside of another aircraft via a rocket-propelled electromagnetic limpet cable. Once in position, the cable transfers the operative in a cradle to the aircraft above.
7. Additional fuel tanks.
8. Entry hatch to pod overhead gallery.
9. Water tank.
10. Twin sleeping bunks.
11. Shower unit.
12. Toilet.
13. Fuel tanks for VTOL ramjets.
14. Hatch to lower storage bay.
15. Air-to-air equipment bay sliding pressure door.
16. Air-to-air equipment personnel safety cradle.
17. Missile firing 'turret' operates topside missile launcher and, if required, the machine cannon located in the equipment deck below.
18. Missile launcher video and range-finder screen.
19. Missile launcher.
20. Missile launcher video and range-finder camera.
21. Multiple doored upper access hatch provides access for pilot's entry chute, passenger lift entry hatch, hover-jets and missile launcher.
22. Pilot's entry chute door.
23. Hover-jet holding bay door.
24. Passenger lift entry hatch.
25. Pilot's entry chute.
26. Medical bay.
27. Casualty monitor screen.
28. Medical bay oxygen cylinders.
29. Medical supply storage.
30. Twin basins.
31. Central access deck and hover-jet holding bay, linking control cabin to missile firing bay, sleeping accommodation, upper storage and air-to-air equipment bays via central corridor.
32. Hover-jets.
33. Pilot's chute control cabin entry hatch.
34. Passenger lift entry point to control cabin.
35. Pilot's seat.
36. Passenger/additional personnel seating.
37. Ergonomically simplified pilot's flight instrument panel.
38. Telemetry computer.
39. Avionics bay.

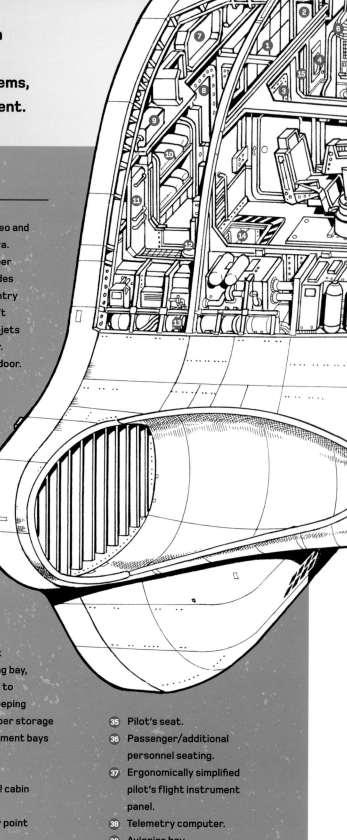

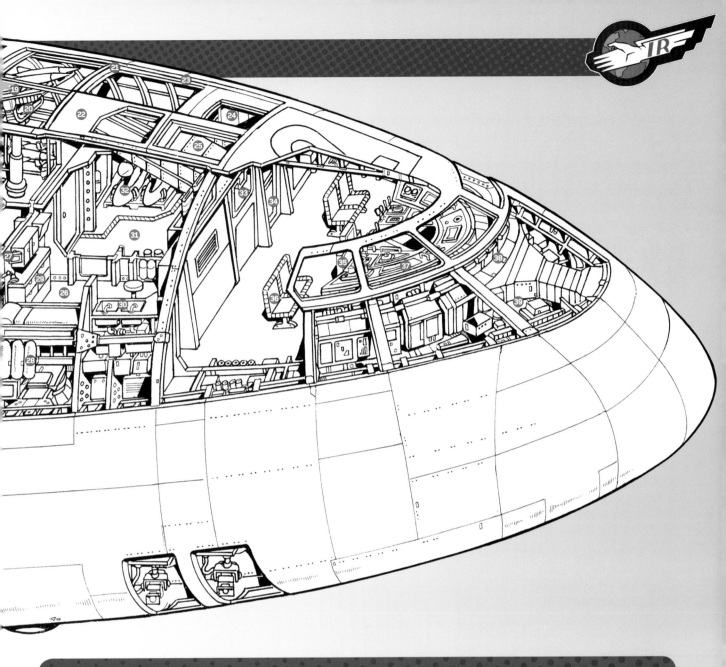

A   Engine diagnostic display screen.

B   Engine control computer.

C   Engine system check-lights.

D   Engine system override control.

E   Communications console.

F   Function activation control.

G   Air-speed indicator.

H   Multi-function video display screen.

I   Elevon and leading edge control pedals.

J   Tail plane fin and rudder pedals.

K   Altitude display.

L   Function selection control.

M   Flight computer override control.

N   Missile control switches.

O   Security system console.

P   Flight system check-lights.

Q   Flight control computer.

R   Flight control systems monitor.

Interchangeable task-specific devices compatible with a centrally mounted winch unit can be selected and lowered from the underside of the nose cone, providing vital operational flexibility.

Equipment deck

1. Access ladder to flight deck.
2. Lift to flight deck.
3. Lower storage bay.
4. Access door from lower storage bay to equipment deck, machine cannon and retro rocket deck, and lift to flight deck.
5. One of two machine cannon fitted with interchangeable ammunition cartridges offering a variety of bullets, anaesthetic darts or shells.
6. Ammunition cartridge.
7. Retro rocket thrust duct.
8. Starboard emergency braking retro rocket.
9. Starboard ramjet air intake.
10. Starboard vertical take-off ramjet.
11. Nozzle outlet.
12. Starboard video camera observation port.
13. Heat-proof rescue cage can carry up to four people.
14. Hydraulic crane swings rescue cage over equipment deck hatch doors when required for rescue operations.
15. Magnetic grab cable reel support beam.
16. Winch cable enables rescue personnel to be lowered precisely into danger zone.
17. Winch ladder with electromagnets.
18. Electromagnetic grabs used for more precise recovery operations.
19. Heavy-duty magnetic grabs primarily used for debris clearance.
20. Set of four cable winch hooks.
21. Hawser cable rocket launcher.
22. Equipment deck bulkhead.
23. Life-support systems access panel.
24. Machine cannon (primarily for demolition).
25. Equipment deck outer hatch.
26. Equipment deck inner hatch.
27. Telemetry computer.
28. Equipment deck manual control console operates the rescue cage, hawser and winch cables, grabs and machine cannon if these cannot be operated from TB2's control cabin.
29. Compressed air tanks.
30. Radar modulator.

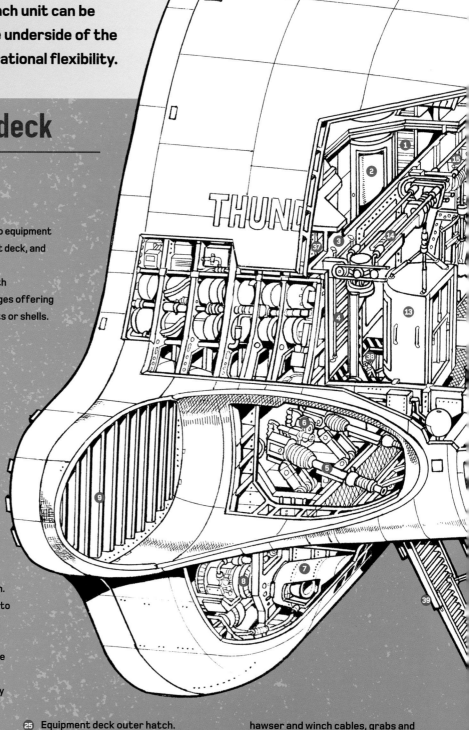

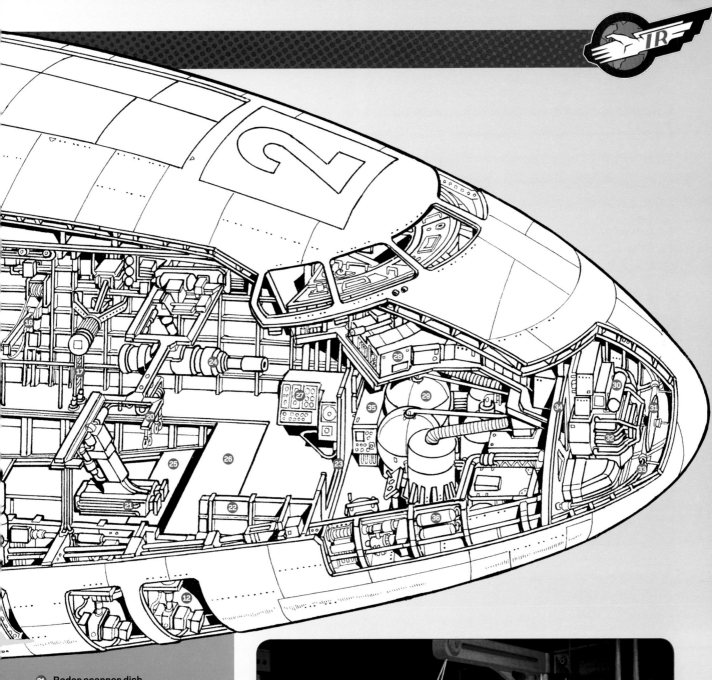

31 Radar scanner dish.

32 MIDAS cloaking system.

33 HALO system.

34 Radar mounting bulkhead.

35 Life-support unit controls
atmosphere recycling, temperature
and also hull cooling systems.

36 Hull cooling systems.

37 Equipment deck exit hatch leading to
pod inspection gallery when TB2 is in
raised position.

38 Access ladder storage well.

39 Access ladder in deployed position,
used by personnel when TB2 is in
lowered position.

Multi-function winch unit: a variety of devices can be selected and operated
via the lower nose cone hatch winch unit to aid in rescue operations.

In addition to three general purpose pods, a laboratory-equipped pod (Pod 5) is available for use on missions. Once Thunderbird 2's launch sequence has been initiated the pods are transported by conveyor to a position directly beneath the craft for incorporation into the main body.

Laboratory pod

1. One of four forward electromagnetic docking clamps that hold the pod in place during flight.
2. Pressure door to Thunderbird 2 flight deck.
3. Strengthened pod door doubles as access ramp for pod vehicles.
4. Forward heavy-duty under carriage rollers.
5. Turntable used for smaller pod vehicles.
6. Laboratory blockhouse.
7. Pod vehicle maintenance and repair crane.
8. Pod power plant fuel cells.
9. Pod laboratory power generator is used if the pod has been detached from Thunderbird 2 and its power systems.
10. Pod power back-up control console. Power from TB2's adjacent reactor to the Pod can be overridden either manually or automatically so that the laboratory can operate using its own generator.
11. Standard pod wall pressurised foam and flame-retardant chemical tanks: used in case of fire in the pod or the vehicles it is carrying.
12. Air conditioning plant.
13. Door to laboratory.

14. View screen, linked to Tracy Island, other International Rescue vehicles, Thunderbird 1's remote camera and external sources.
15. Workbench.
16. Additional workbench facilities plus storage.
17. Large laboratory door used if bigger items or components need attention in laboratory conditions.
18. To maximise the available space inside the pod, some vehicles can be vertically 'stacked' on the pod vehicle storage platform. When the vehicle below has been driven out, the platform is lowered at the door-facing end so that the vehicle above can be deployed.
19. Storage platform lift hydraulics.

20. Ramp lowers to allow vehicle on platform to be driven off.
21. Recovery vehicle storage position. On arrival at the danger zone this vehicle is driven out of the pod first, followed by the vehicle on the top deck. After the mission, the vehicle on the top deck is reversed in first and clamped into position.

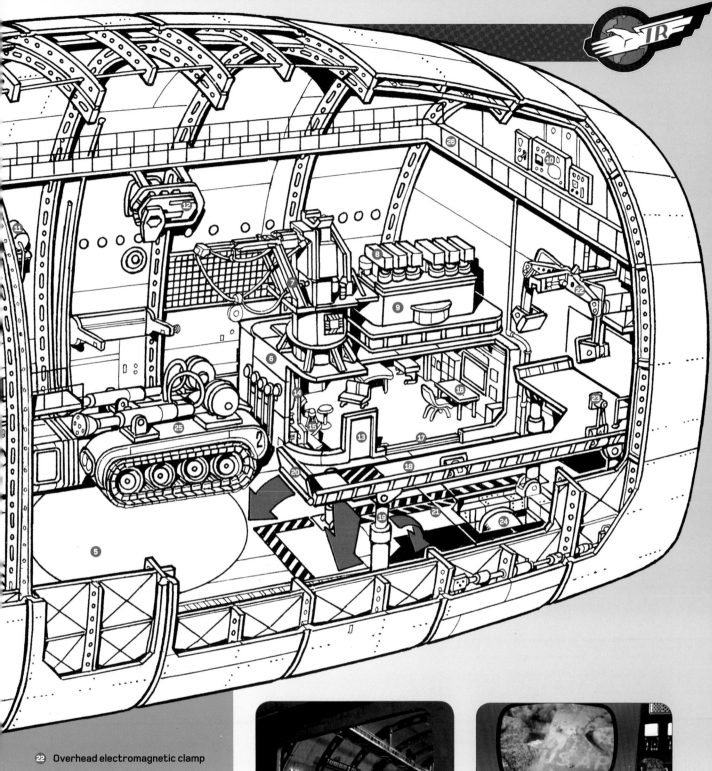

22 Overhead electromagnetic clamp prevents pod vehicle movement during Thunderbird 2's flight to and from the danger zone.

23 Pod vehicle side clamps.

24 Rear heavy-duty undercarriage rollers.

25 One of the two remote-control recovery vehicles.

26 Inspection gallery.

Pod inspection walkway: access between Thunderbird 2 nose cone and pod when main body has been raised is possible by means of the pod inspection walkway.

Pod laboratory: Pod 5 is fitted with a small laboratory which allows Brains to carry out essential experiments during the course of a mission.

P od 2 is equipped with a powerful set of mechanical grabs designed for lifting precariously positioned objects or vehicles, and operate in magnetic or suction-assisted mode. The pod also contains a pressurised hover-powered mobile control centre for use in hostile environments.

Pod 2

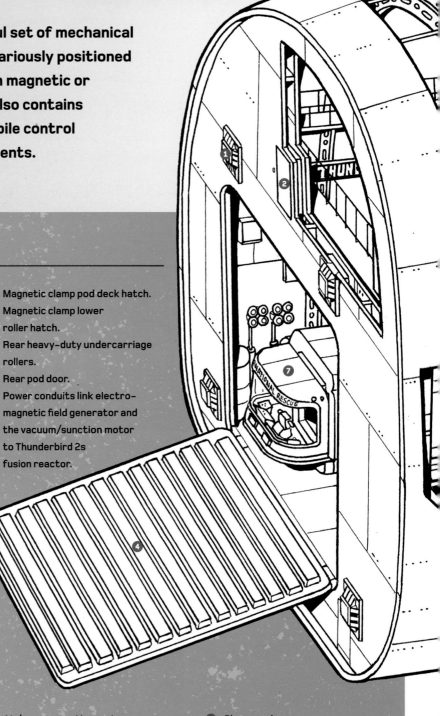

1 One of four forward electromagnetic docking clamps that hold the pod in place during flight.

2 Pressure door to Thunderbird 2 flight deck.

3 Pod overhead inspection gallery.

4 Strengthened pod door doubles as access ramp for pod vehicles.

5 Forward heavy-duty undercarriage rollers.

6 Inner stressed wall in all pods provides maximum strength to the pod's lightweight construction.

7 Mobile command centre. When Thunderbird 1's mobile control unit cannot be used for extreme heat, poisonous atmosphere or high-radiation conditions, the mobile command centre provides a self-contained and hermetically sealed alternative. The hover unit contains all the resources needed to oversee a rescue operation, including a small laboratory, air-locked doors and a decontamination unit. All the features found on the mobile control unit are also duplicated here.

8 Magnetic clamp pod deck hatch.

9 Magnetic clamp lower roller hatch.

10 Rear heavy-duty undercarriage rollers.

11 Rear pod door.

12 Power conduits link electromagnetic field generator and the vacuum/sunction motor to Thunderbird 2s fusion reactor.

13 Air/vacuum suction motor produces a vacuum seal on each clamp grab if the surface being adhered to is flat.

14 Electromagnetic field generator.

15 Motor inspection/maintenance platform.

16 Telescopic clamp support column.

17 Clamp grab pressure hydraulics.

18 Magnetic clamp support frame.

19 Auxilliary magnetic clamp control console.

20 Electromagnetic clamp grabs.

21 Vacuum seal nozzles.

22 Grab adjustable angle pivot.

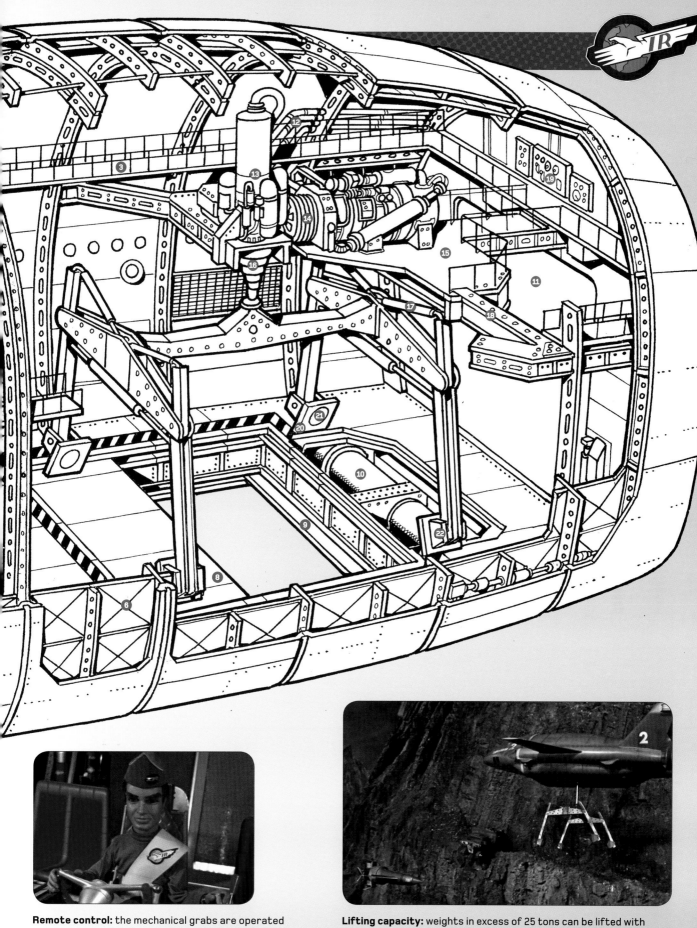

Remote control: the mechanical grabs are operated from the multi-function control lever in the cockpit.

Lifting capacity: weights in excess of 25 tons can be lifted with the aid of the mechanical grabs and then flown to safety.

THUNDERBIRD 3

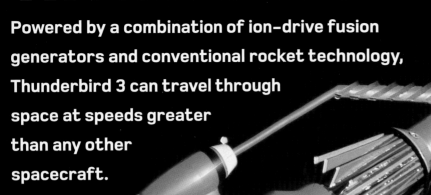

Powered by a combination of ion-drive fusion generators and conventional rocket technology, Thunderbird 3 can travel through space at speeds greater than any other spacecraft.

Thunderbird 3
Technical data

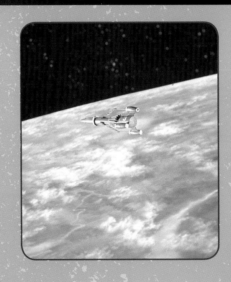

DIMENSIONS
LENGTH: 287 feet
NACELLE SPAN: 80 feet
DIAMETER: 23 feet
WEIGHT: 562 tons

PERFORMANCE
LAUNCH THRUST:
4.5 million pounds
STANDARD ACCELERATION: 1g
MAXIMUM SUSTAINED ACCELERATION: 6g
EMERGENCY ACCELERATION: 10g
RANGE: Unlimited

POWER
POWER SOURCE: Atomic fusion reactor

ENGINES: 3 chemical rockets used for launch, landing, emergency boost and orbit change; 3 ion-drive particle accelerators used in deep space
PITCH AND YAW ROCKETS: 12 in middle ring for course corrections, 20 in nose and 24 at rear for attitude adjustment

TECHNOLOGY DATA FILE

Although its use in space rescue missions has so far been comparatively infrequent, Thunderbird 3 plays an essential part in International Rescue's operational management. Originally built to enable construction of Thunderbird 5 to be carried out in space, the giant rocket now provides a regular shuttle service to the satellite, transporting essential supplies and allowing the station to be manned by alternate crews on a monthly basis.

With an outer hull fabricated from a super-hardened compound of Cahelium Extract X incorporating ceramic additives, the craft's central fuselage is offset by three fin-mounted thruster units, which also serve to support the ship on its launch pad.

The main crew quarters are built into a self-contained module located in the nose cone of the ship and surrounded by a secondary skin to provide meteor protection. Access to the module during the launch procedure on Tracy Island is via the mobile couch transit tube, which forms the central core of the vehicle. The couch terminates in the lower take-off lounge, from which a turbo lift gives access to a sleeping cabin, stores area and control deck in the upper part of the module, and to a space equipment storage bay and service airlock located beneath the lounge. This area can also be accessed by an extending gantry in the craft's launch silo for maintenance and loading of supplies.

Power for Thunderbird 3 during take-off and for supplementary flight boost is supplied by conventional chemical rockets fuelled by Monatomic propellant stored in Helium pressurised tanks. Primary spaceflight propulsion is powered by twin ion-drive fusion generators. These are positioned in the centre of the ship and feed particle drive guns mounted in the three extended thruster fins. A stream of charged particles is created, driving the ship forward at top speeds that remain unverified. This revolutionary process provided the only means of rescuing the imperilled Sun Probe rocket during its recent near-disastrous solar exploration mission.

Directional control of the craft during atmospheric flight is maintained with forward, rear and centrally mounted pitch and yaw rockets. Additional control in space can be achieved through the use of a dual-flywheel generator assembly. For docking with Thunderbird 5, sensors mounted in the vacuum sealing ring forward of the lower airlock provide ultra precise vector guidance factoring. Once docked, a boarding gangway is clamped to the nose cone allowing direct entry to Thunderbird 5's control areas and living quarters.

Astronaut
Thunderbird 3
Alan Tracy

AREA OF SPECIALISATION
Space rescue, Thunderbird 2 back-up crew and alternating space monitor

BACKGROUND
Alan's teenage fascination with space travel led to a near catastrophic accident when an experimental rocket project he was involved with while studying at Colorado University resulted in unexpected disaster. Having learnt from this early mistake, Alan went on to prove himself a capable astronaut with several lunar missions to his credit. His love of speed is also reflected in his involvement with motor racing, and he gave up a promising career in the sport to focus on his life in International Rescue.

PERSONAL CHARACTERISTICS
A keen sportsman who enjoys rock climbing and running, Alan finds the challenge of exploring the more inaccessible parts of Tracy Island a constant source of adrenalin-inducing activity. The youngest of the Tracy brothers, Alan formed a close bond with Tin-Tin at an early age, but both are careful not to let this affect their roles in International Rescue.

nternational Rescue's space rescue and satellite shuttle craft.

Overview

1. Forward sensor array detects debris ahead of the craft so that course corrections can be made using the pitch and yaw rockets.
2. Forward pitch and yaw course correction rockets.
3. Pitch and yaw rocket fuel tanks.
4. Pitch and yaw rocket attachment ring.
5. Pressurised dome bulkhead.
6. Navigation and telemetry computers.
7. MIDAS anti-detection system.
8. Flight deck.
9. Ergonomically simplified flight console maintains Thunderbird 3's control systems allowing pilot to concentrate on course correction and manoeuvring procesdures.
10. Outer airlock hatch provides access from the flight deck to Thunderbird 5's docking bay. The airlock, and Thunderbird 5's docking bay access ramp, is gravity variable enabling the pilot to be reorientated with Thunderbird 5's gravity systems, which are at 90 degrees to Thunderbird 3's gravity direction.
11. Inner airlock door provides access to flight deck.
12. Turbo lift hatch.

13. Main view screen linked to hull cameras and telemetry data computer systems.
14. Secondary computer monitor screen.
15. Artificial gravity control box.
16. Life-support and air-recycling systems.
17. Oxygen tanks.
18. Flight deck temperature regulation systems.
19. One of two airlocks linking the flight deck to Thunderbird 5 or to open space if necessary. Also can be accessed from adjacent turbo lift and emergency access tunnel.
20. Storage bay.
21. Central storage units contain spacesuit helmets, emergency breathing apparatus, survival equipment, medical supplies, food and water.
22. Outer ring storage units contain spacesuits, oxygen tanks and rescue equipment.
23. Storage bay lift door to emergency access tunnel.
24. Storage bay lift door.
25. Sleeping quarters if required on longer journeys.
26. Twin bunks.
27. Emergency supplies storage lockers.

28. Toilet and shower, both with zero-gravity operating systems.
29. Lounge deck.
30. Tracy villa lounge couch atop entry tunnel.
31. Radio safety beam transmitter console.
32. One of three lift off/acceleration couches for use by additional personel.
33. Emergency access tunnel runs alongside turbo lift providing access to all decks in the event of power failure. Lift doors can be manually overridden to gain entry to the decks in these circumstances.
34. Artificial gravity generating ring built into the decks of all levels.
35. Shielded entry tunnel with integrated emergency ladder built into interior tunnel walls.

Flight control: a compact flight deck allows Thunderbird 3 to be piloted by one person.

Equipment bay: Thunderbird 3's crew can carry out space rescues from the lower deck storage bay.

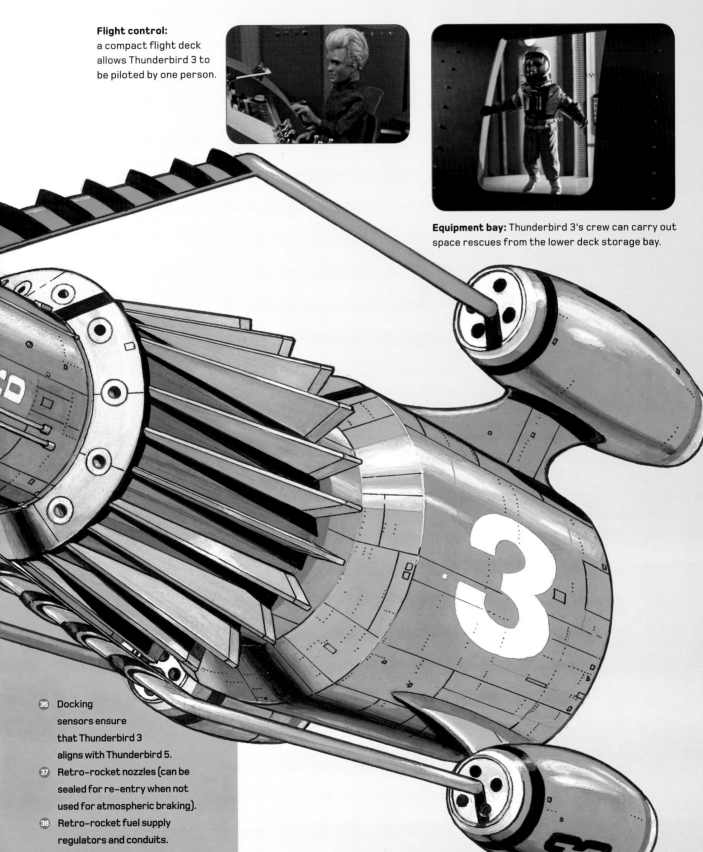

36 Docking sensors ensure that Thunderbird 3 aligns with Thunderbird 5.

37 Retro-rocket nozzles (can be sealed for re-entry when not used for atmospheric braking).

38 Retro-rocket fuel supply regulators and conduits.

Thunderbird 3 is powered by chemical propellant and Ion-drive particle acceleration guns supplying three dual-function thruster units. Super-cooled atomic fusion generation is employed to charge the particle accelerators.

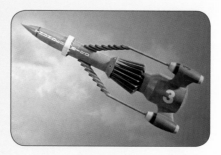

Return flight: on its return to base, computer guidance systems enable Thunderbird 3 to position itself in mid-air for vertical landing.

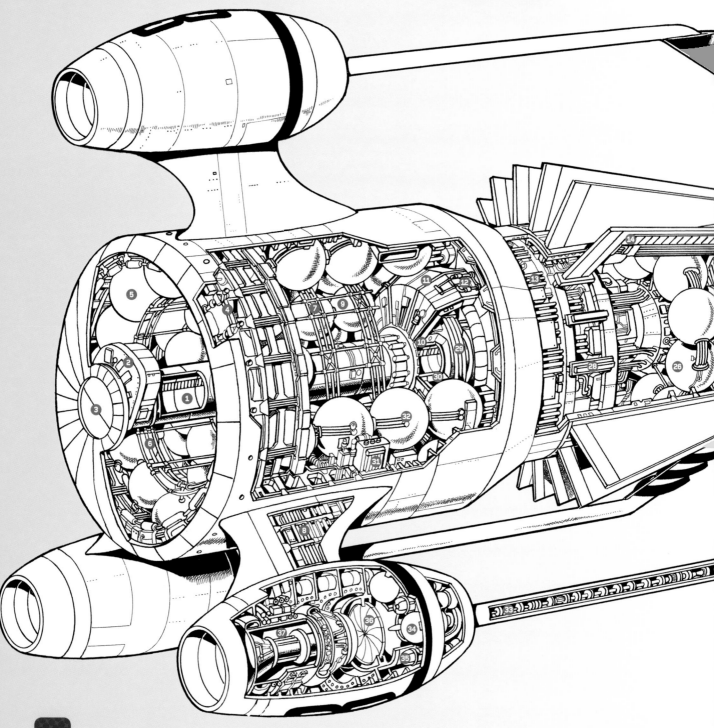

Propulsion and power

1. Entry tunnel.
2. Entry Tunnel airlock.
3. Entry Tunnel air lock door: the couch from the Tracy Villa is raised on a hydraulic ram up through the entry tunnel prior to launch. Once the couch is locked into position, the ram retracts and the airlock is closed.
4. Rear pitch and yaw rockets.
5. Helium pressurised monoatomic propellant tanks for main motors.
6. Propellant tank attachment inner frame.
7. Propellant tank attachment points.
8. Control and fuel lines from propellant tanks.
9. Inner propellant tank ring.
10. Inner tunnel shielding.
11. Toughened cahelium and graphite reactor shielding.
12. Reactor management control systems.
13. Reactor cooling ducts.
14. Radiant cooling intake fins cool the generator via cooling ducts.
15. Hull bulkhead frame.
16. Dual-flywheel motor assemblage: attitude alteration is achieved by spinning the twin flywheels in opposite directions, supplementing the pitch and yaw and retro rockets located at the rare of the craft, the central ring, docking ring and nose.
17. Tractor beam guidance sensor enables Thunderbird 3 to land safely in its hangar below the Round House on Tracy Island.
18. Docking ring fuel lines.
19. Docking ring retro rocket fuel tanks.
20. Fuselage/Ion accelerator spar main frame.
21. Fuel lines from tanks to central ring.
22. Attitude control rockets, vector able for roll, pitch and yaw corrections, used in conjunction with adjacent flywheel.
23. Ion accelerator spar.
24. Re-entry heat dissipation vanes.
25. Central ring.
26. Ring of electricity generators powered by the fusion reactor provide power for the Ion drive and life support systems.
27. Ion-drive particle gun: once escape velocity has been achieved, each particle gun provides continuous acceleration with an exhaust stream of charged atomic particles.
28. Cooling fin attachment members.
29. Ion-drive atomic fusion generator.
30. Shielded entry chute.
31. Fuel management systems and electronics.
32. Fuel valves.
33. Particle accelerator.
34. Retro rocket fuel tanks.
35. Chemical retro rockets.
36. Gate seal blocks off particle accelerator from explosion chamber when rockets are firing.
37. Chemical rocket explosion chamber for take-off and additional boost.

Space walk: the crew are equipped to perform ship-to-ship space walks and external repairs.

Turbo lift: the crew decks of Thunderbird 3 are accessed by an internal turbo-lift.

THUNDERBIRD 4

Underwater rescue craft equipped
with multi-function tools

Thunderbird 4
Technical data

DIMENSIONS
LENGTH: 30 feet
WIDTH: 11 feet
WEIGHT: 16 tons

PERFORMANCE
UNDERWATER SPEED: 160 knots
**SURFACE CRUISING
SPEED:** 40 knots
**EMERGENCY LAUNCH
SPEED:** 30 knots
**MAXIMUM OPERATING
DEPTH:** 30,000 feet

POWER
POWER SOURCE: Twin atomic
fusion reactors
FORWARD AND REVERSE DRIVE:
6 electrically driven reversible
axial-flow turbine impellers
MAIN TURBO DRIVE: 2 axial-flow
turbines providing forward
thrust only
EMERGENCY LAUNCH JETS:
4 vertical-thrust hover-jets and
2 x 25 liquid fuel mini-rockets

TECHNOLOGY DATA FILE

The smallest of the five Thunderbird craft, Thunderbird 4 is a vital and operationally well proven part of the International Rescue fleet. Compact, yet immensely strong, the craft has been built to withstand the pressures of the deepest oceans, and can carry out complex underwater tasks with the aid of a forward-mounted range of tools.

Twin atomic mini-pile fusion generators power the craft. A larger unit positioned amidships supplies the six main drive impellers housed in the side- and top-mounted nacelles, and is supplemented by a smaller secondary unit towards the stern which powers auxiliary systems and superheats air for surface drive propulsion and emergency launch hover-jets. Additional miniature rocket boosters may be engaged to provide launch boost or forward motion when in hover mode.

Control of the craft is from a small cabin fitted with a panoramic Cahelium and Formula C/31 additive strengthened Armourglass screen. Further upper visibility is provided by a cabin roof viewport of the same material. Access to the craft can be made either through a telescopic autolock built into the port side of the cabin, or through roof-mounted hatches opening into an airlock positioned between the cabin and engine room.

Oxygen and life support systems can be found immediately forward of the cabin, with the prow of the ship containing a quadri-barrelled tool bar fitted with a selection of devices. The two outer units house powerful telescopic rams, which can be magnetised to grip trapped or disabled vessels. A third unit is fitted with mini torpedoes for use in underwater demolition operations, while the remaining unit contains a variety of tools including a grapple arm, directional laser cutter and a harpoon drill connected to a flexible hose. This can be used to pump oxygen into stranded vessels or, if the occupants are hostile, knock-out gas. Illumination to aid underwater operations is mounted in an adjustable parabolic reflector unit forward of the tool bar, which can be positioned above or below the prow. Additional equipment in the stern of the craft includes a magnetic clamp attachment for towing other vessels or subsidiary rescue equipment.

When required for a mission Thunderbird 4 is usually airlifted to the danger zone by Thunderbird 2 in Pod 4. Alternatively, the craft may be launched from Tracy Island using the onboard hover-jets and the tilting ramp built into the end of the island's runway.

Aquanaut
Thunderbird 4
Gordon Tracy

AREA OF SPECIALISATION
Underwater rescues, Thunderbird 2 back-up crew.

BACKGROUND
Unlike his brothers, Gordon found himself drawn to inner space rather than outer space having developed an early interest in aquatic exploration and oceanography. A champion Olympic swimmer and former member of the Submarine Service and World Aquanaut Security Patrol, he has an expert knowledge of marine biology, having spent a year studying advanced undersea farming methods while in command of a deep-sea bathyscape. His experience and respect for the sea made him the perfect choice to pilot Thunderbird 4. He is also an expert marksman and possess rock-steady nerves.

PERSONAL CHARACTERISTICS
The joker of the five Tracy boys, Gordon often finds himself at odds with his father, who does not appreciate his flippant sense of humour. Off duty he enjoys chess, fishing and playing the guitar.

THUNDERBIRD 4

A mini submarine capable of withstanding immense oceanic pressure, Thunderbird 4 is equipped to carry out a wide range of tasks that may be required to effect a successful underwater rescue.

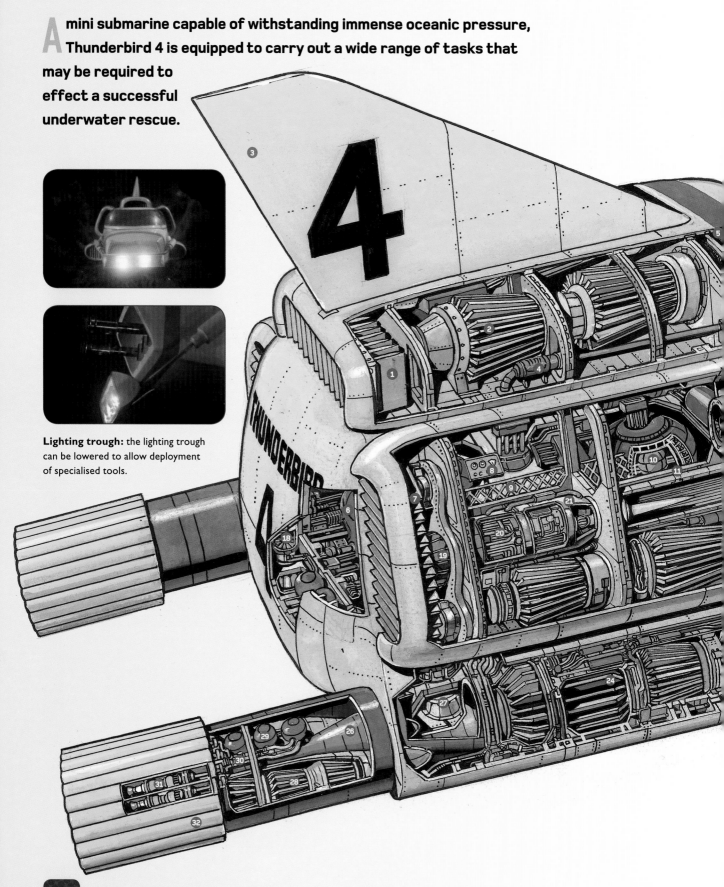

Lighting trough: the lighting trough can be lowered to allow deployment of specialised tools.

TB4 Overview

1. Rear top nacelle steering vanes – can be closed to form an airtight seal if necessary.

2. One of six electrically driven reversible axial–flow impellers – two in each nacelle .

3. Stabilising fin.

4. Starboard top nacelle water and air pump: used to cool reactors or to pump air into nacelles in an emergency.

5. Forward top nacelle steering vanes and anti–debris filter.

6. Atomic fusion generator powers auxilliaries, and superheats air for surface jet engines and hover–jets.

7. Rear starboard nacelle steering vanes control surfacing and diving.

8. Gantry mounted atomic systems monitor – duplicated on cabin control console.

9. Starboard crawl–through turbine and fusion generator maintenance gantry.

10. Primary atomic fusion generator provides power for axial–flow impellers.

11. Watertight inner nacelle bulkhead wall.

12. Topside airlock hatch doors.

13. Airlock control systems and air regulator.

14. Watertight access door to pilot's cabin.

15. Airlock water drainage grille.

16. Forward starboard vertical thrust hover–jet. If Thunderbird 2 is out of action, Thunderbird 4 can be launched from Pod 4 in its hangar on Tracy Island.

17. Hover–jet water tight doors.

18. Rear port vertical thrust hover–jet.

19. Gate–sealed jet engine thrust pipe.

20. Starboard nacelle jet engine turbine. Used for surface cruising and sealed watertight when Thunderbird 4 is submerged.

21. Jet engine sealed ducting.

22. Jet engine intake and gate seal.

23. Forward water intakes and steering vanes.

24. Starboard main drive electrically driven axial–flow turbine.

25. Starboard turbine anti–debris grille.

26. Axial–flow turbine thrust pipe.

27. Rear starboard vertical thrust hover–jet.

28. Auxiliary axial flow impellers.

29. Rocket fuel tanks.

30. Control lines and rocket fuel pumps.

31. Starboard rocket battery nacelle. Rockets are used to launch Thunderbird 4 from Pod 4 on the surface of the water or from the hangar.

32. Sealable rocket thrust pipes.

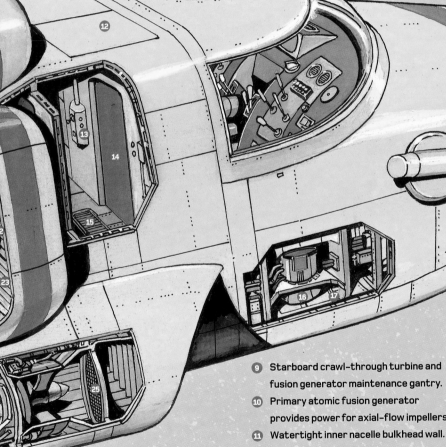

THUNDERBIRD 4

Thunderbird 4 is piloted from a central control position fitted with a panoramic viewing screen. This gives excellent visibility for carrying out underwater rescue work with the aid of forward mounted devices.

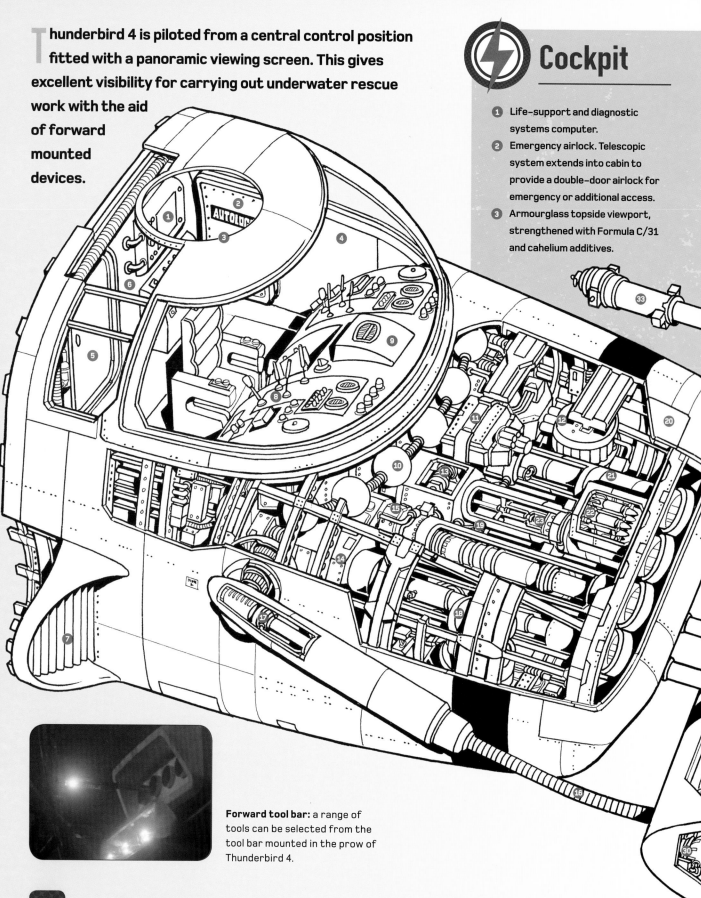

Cockpit

1. Life-support and diagnostic systems computer.
2. Emergency airlock. Telescopic system extends into cabin to provide a double-door airlock for emergency or additional access.
3. Armourglass topside viewport, strengthened with Formula C/31 and cahelium additives.

Forward tool bar: a range of tools can be selected from the tool bar mounted in the prow of Thunderbird 4.

4 Main viewport provides 180-degree visibility for pilot, strengthened with Formula C/31 and cahelium.

5 Access door to topside airlock.

6 Fire extinguisher.

7 Starboard turbine water intake.

8 Control instrument panel.

9 Multi-function video screen.

10 Oxygen tanks.

11 Life-support unit with zyolithic crystal converter to eliminate the build up of carbon dioxide in the cabin.

12 Pod re-entry electromagnetic docking clamp.

13 Drill cable with built-in oxygen tube.

14 Ram hydraulics electric motor.

15 Laser beam generator.

16 Multi-jointed arm enables flexible positioning of the reflector trough.

17 Servo mechanism controls reflector trough positioning.

18 Starboard forward pod re-entry electro-magnetic docking clamp (see Pod 4 re-entry system).

19 Adjustment sprocket allows tool tubes to be raised enabling equipment to be substituted prior to a rescue operation.

20 Tool tube access panel.

21 One of four tool tubes.

22 Missile auto-loader.

23 If a missile is not loaded into the tool tube, a harpoon-drill can be fired. The drill is linked via tube to the auxilliary oxygen tanks and can be used to pump air into a downed submarine.

24 Port hydraulic ram.

25 Demolition missile.

26 Laser cutter.

27 Multi-jointed laser cutter arm enables the arm to be used accurately.

28 Electro-magnetic clamp incorporated into hydraulic ram head.

29 Port sensor array.

30 Starboard sonar dish.

31 Parabolic reflector trough, shown in lowered position to enable on board rescue equipment to be used.

32 Halogen lighting bar.

33 Optional grappling arm: depending on the rescue requirements, any of the rescue tools at the front of Thunderbird 4 can be substituted for specialised equipment prior to launch, via the tool tube access panel.

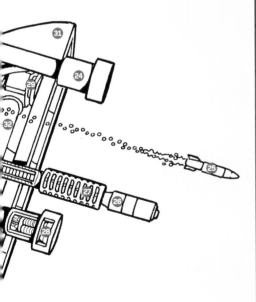

A Surface jet indicator lights.

B Port air circulation vent.

C Laser cutter activation control lever.

D Upper hatch control lever.

E Atmosphere and life-support display.

F Missile activation control.

G Life-support control systems.

H Surface jet activation control.

I Port ram and laser extender controls.

J Monitor display selector.

K Impeller control pedals.

L Multi-function display monitor.

M Magnetic ram and grapple controls.

N Tool bar function selector.

O Hover-jet activation control.

P Ballast control systems.

Q Air-hose drill activation lever.

R Atomic power plant status display.

S Lighting control lever.

T Lighting bar position control lever.

U Starboard air circulation vent.

V Hover-jet indicator lights.

T hunderbird 4 is usually launched from Thunderbird 2's Pod 4, which is fitted with a sliding ramp and magnetic clamp craft-retrieval system.

Ocean launch: Thunderbird 4 can be launched in mid-ocean from the floating pod.

Pod 4

1. One of four forward electro-magnetic docking clamps that hold the Pod in place during flight.
2. Pressure door to Thunderbird 2 flight deck.
3. Pod overhead inspection gallery.
4. Air conditioning plant.
5. Strengthened pod door doubles as access ramp for pod vehicles or launch ramp support for Thunderbird 4.
6. Forward bouyancy tank.
7. Forward heavy-duty undercarriage rollers.
8. Midships bouyancy tank.
9. Thunderbird 4 launch ramp in raised position.
10. Launch ramp hydraulic lift ram.
11. Thunderbird 4 recovery clamps.
12. High pressure pumps remove water from Pod 4 in rough weather whilst the pod door is open.
13. Rear bouyancy tank.

14. Rear heavy-duty undercarriage rollers.

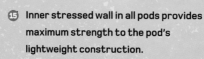

15. Inner stressed wall in all pods provides maximum strength to the pod's lightweight construction.
16. Underwater sealing unit primarily used to contain natural gas eruptions on the seabed. The unit is towed by Thunderbird 4 into position and is lowered over the eruption.

17. Sealing unit ballast valves.
18. Sealing unit launch trolley.
19. Sealing unit trolley sliding launch rail built into ramp extension. Both the ramp extension and sealing unit are not normally stowed in Pod 4 unless a rescue operation demands it.

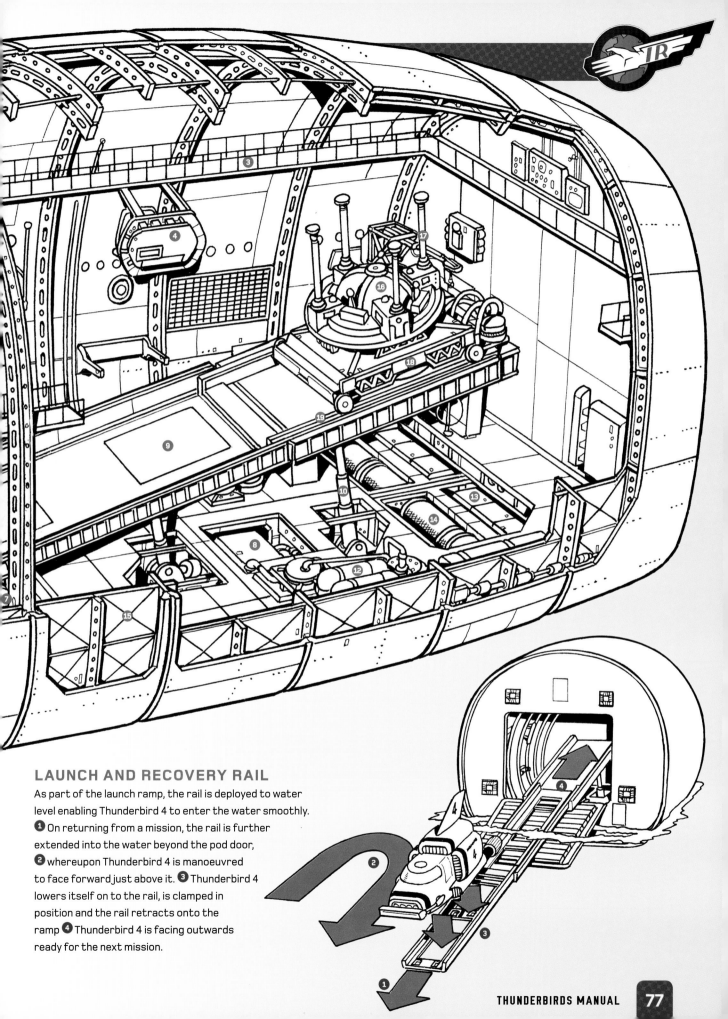

LAUNCH AND RECOVERY RAIL

As part of the launch ramp, the rail is deployed to water level enabling Thunderbird 4 to enter the water smoothly. ❶ On returning from a mission, the rail is further extended into the water beyond the pod door, ❷ whereupon Thunderbird 4 is manoeuvred to face forward just above it. ❸ Thunderbird 4 lowers itself on to the rail, is clamped in position and the rail retracts onto the ramp ❹ Thunderbird 4 is facing outwards ready for the next mission.

THUNDERBIRD 5

Thunderbird 5 maintains watch above the Earth, constantly monitoring all communication wavelengths.

Thunderbird 5
Technical data

DIMENSIONS
LENGTH: 400 feet
WINGSPAN: 272 feet
DIAMETER: 296 feet
WEIGHT: 976 tons

PERFORMANCE
RECEPTION RANGE: 100 million miles
ORBIT: Geo-stationary 22,400 miles above the Pacific Ocean

POWER
POWER SOURCE: Atomic batteries
GRAVITY: Previn Coil artificial gravity generator: Earth standard (with options)

TECHNOLOGY DATA FILE

The electronic eyes and ears of the International Rescue organisation, Thunderbird 5 maintains a geo-stationary position beyond the orbits of commercial and military satellites.

Constructed in space over the course of two years, the vessel consists of two main sections: a three-deck hub housing a power plant and crew facilities, and a subsidiary docking arm built to accommodate Thunderbird 3. The spacecraft makes monthly visits to Thunderbird 5, ferrying supplies and allowing for crew alternation.

The space station's power is derived primarily from banks of atomic batteries installed on the lower deck. These are recharged monthly by Thunderbird 3's fusion generators. Emergency solar reserve power is also available. The mid-hub deck is allocated to crew accommodation including a lounge, galley dining area, sleeping cabins and stores. On the upper deck are duplicate monitor rooms to ensure 24-hour reception and transmission is maintained during servicing or in the event of technical malfunction. This deck also incorporates a duty monitor cabin, medical bay and emergency airlock. An additional feature of the central hub, situated above the upper deck, is a transparent astrodome housing a powerful radio telescope fitted with manual or remote viewing functions. The three hub decks are connected by tubular passageways served by a turbo-lift, which also connect the hub to the docking arm.

To protect the station from the danger of meteor strikes, a plasma-cored deflector ring surrounds the main hub. This creates an effective screen against most forms of space debris. Additional protection is provided by double-skinned outer panels filled with a coagulant compound to seal micro-punctures in the event of deflector failure. Equally important to the effective operation of Thunderbird 5 is a fail-safe anti-detection shield. This is provided by a ring of electromagnetic baffles installed on the base of the hub, capable of generating a negative radar image for the space station on even the most advanced scanners.

Most essential to the role played by Thunderbird 5 in International Rescue's missions is the satellite's communication system. Central to the reception of messages from any part of the world is the high powered base antenna. This is positioned at the end of an extended pylon to prevent distortion of signals by the anti-meteor deflector and security shield baffles. Worldwide reception is made possible through links to subsidiary receiver/transmitters built into the Tracy Corporation's chain of weather satellites, and by a network of concealed ground booster stations. Once received by Thunderbird 5, signals are filtered by a sophisticated bank of language translation computers sensitive to vocal stress modulation patterns. These ensure that only the most genuine sounding distress calls are brought to the attention of the duty monitor. Messages can then be relayed directly to Tracy Island by the satellite's special frequency scanner ensuring immediate response to the request, 'Calling International Rescue ...'.

Space Monitor
Thunderbird 5
John Tracy

AREA OF SPECIALISATION
Communications and navigation systems. Alternates with Alan as pilot of Thunderbird 3 and as Thunderbird 2 back-up crew.

BACKGROUND
Harvard educated, where he studied astro-communications, John was the first of the Tracy brothers to qualify as an astronaut and to follow his father's footsteps into space. An expert astronomer, his discovery of a new quasar system came as the result of his ceaseless quest to learn more about the universe.

PERSONAL CHARACTERISTICS
Sharp-minded and possessing great mental energy, John can at times seem over enthusiastic and lacking in caution, but his ability to quickly assess a situation proves invaluable in dealing with distress calls. In his spare time he has written several books about astronomy and space exploration.

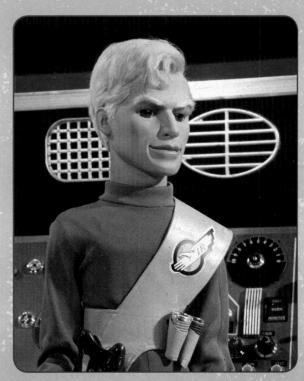

THUNDERBIRD 5

Stationed far above the Earth, Thunderbird 5 constantly monitors global communications with the aid of sophisticated multi-waveband receivers. Signals can be immediately translated and filtered for attention by the duty monitor.

TB5 Overview

1. Moveable screens cover windows from sun glare.
2. Access hatch leading to Thunderbird 5's duplicate control room. This is used if the main control room is damaged or out of action. Computer systems are independently powered by the adjacent solar energy panels and all data is duplicated from the primary systems.
3. Spare signalling laser beam system and star-fix sensors used to maintain Thunderbird 5's orbital position.
4. Radiation-shielded astrodome housing telescope and near space monitoring systems. Polarised multi-layered 'intelligent' quartz glass automatically reduces solar glare.
5. Anti-glare baffles.
6. High powered optical telescope with wide field/planetary camera.
7. Solar energy panels.
8. Medical bay.
9. Airlock doors leading to spare scanners maintenance platform and lift to lower deck and docking bay.
10. Primary monitor/control room.
11. Main monitor console linked to language translation computer programmes that filters and records all messages containing words such as 'emergency' or 'help'.
12. Multi-system audio recordng system.
13. Thunderbird 5's orbital positioning override unit.

14. Access ladder to astrodome.
15. Life-support systems control console.
16. Spacesuit storage locker.
17. Handheld rescue/maintenance equipment.
18. Coded frequency antenna maintains electronic or audio visual communications with Tracy Island.
19. External environment sensor array measures radiation and solar wind.
20. Central corridor leading to lift at docking bay end and ladder leading to astrodome at the other.
21. Thunderbird 5's control console used to alter the satellite's orbital position.
22. Turbo lift to all decks.
23. Thunderbird 5's monitors sleeping accommodation and study.
24. Lounge.
25. Mobile electronic entertainment system console: features a library of movies, music control system and games console.
26. Door leading to accommodation deck rooms including laboratory, additional sleeping quarters, storage rooms and hydroponics bay.
27. Sealed shower unit.

28. Personal hygiene station incorporates shower and toilet that can be used in zero gravity.
29. Shielded atomic fusion power generator.
30. Artificial gravity generator.
31. Oxygen tanks.
32. Additional air tanks.
33. Air mixture and circulation processors.
34. One of six electromagnetic anti-detection cloaking baffles prevent the accidental discovery of Thunderbird 5 by radar.
35. Plasma-covered localised field meteor deflector.
36. Plasma pumps serving the meteor deflector.
37. One of four field magnetic pole units.
38. Life-support generators linked to hydroponics system and powered by adjacent fusion reactor.
39. Main monitoring antenna held clear of the anti detection field on a long pylon.

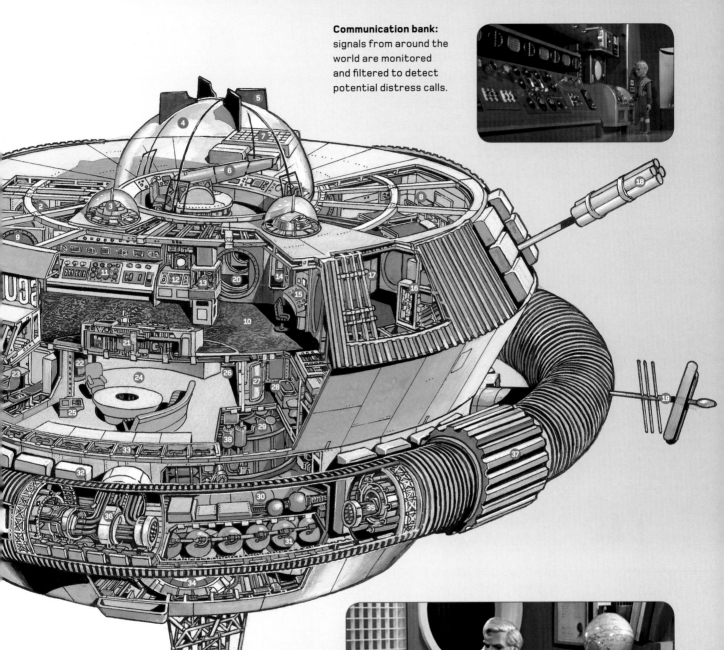

Communication bank: signals from around the world are monitored and filtered to detect potential distress calls.

Crew quarters: the upper deck of Thunderbird 5 provides crew accommodation for the duty monitor.

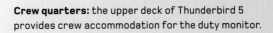

To allow unrestricted access between Thunderbirds 3 and 5, a sealable docking port has been built into an arm extending from the satellite. The arm also serves as a mounting point for twin-gate space antennae.

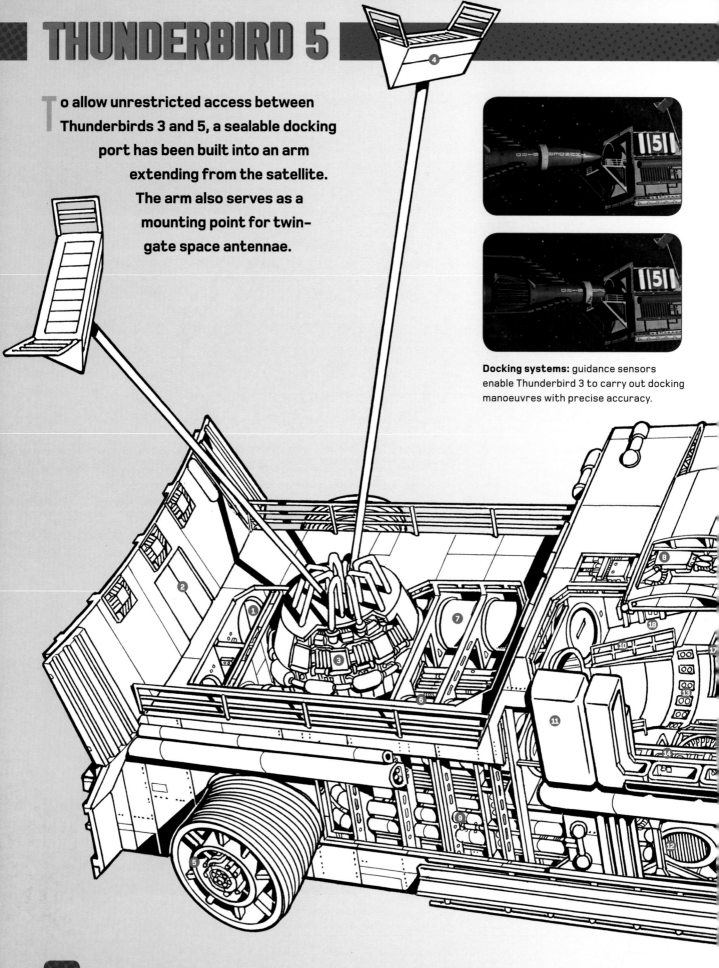

Docking systems: guidance sensors enable Thunderbird 3 to carry out docking manoeuvres with precise accuracy.

 # Docking bay

1. Entrance to Thunderbird 5's main body on living quarters level.
2. Airlock on Thunderbird 5's control level enables maintenance to be carried out on the space scanners power systems.
3. Space scanners power and amplification systems.
4. Twin-gate space scanners; used to detect meteors and monitor communications.
5. Part of the plasma cored localised field meteor deflector ring.
6. Port docking tunnel.
7. Starboard docking tunnel.
8. Retracted fuel feed pumps for Thunderbird 3.
9. Air conduits linking oxygen tanks and life-support units in the main body of Thunderbird 5 to the docking bay, either when Thunderbird 3 is docked, or when the docking bay hatch is closed.
10. Handrails help disembarking personnel from Thunderbird 3 reorientate themselves with Thunderbird 5's adjusted gravity direction.
11. Rocket fuel tanks for Thunderbird 3 if refuelling is required.
12. Heat dispersal unit.
13. Thunderbird 3 nose cone sensors.
14. Fuel pumps.
15. Platform airlock.
16. Thunderbird 3 docking port. When docked, the white docking ring on Thunderbird 3 clamps into position forming an airtight seal.
17. Variable localised gravity generator enables disembarking personnel from Thunderbird 3 to reorientate themselves to Thunderbird 5's change of gravity direction when entering the docking bay's weightless environment. Gravity is gradually introduced so that they can enter the docking tunnel normally.
18. One of two access ramps running alongside Thunderbird 3's nose airlocks when docked. Ramp slopes downwards to docking tunnel and airlocks opening out at living quarters level.
19. Docking bay outer hatch. To save on air in an area not used very often the docking bay is left open to the vacuum of space, but can be closed for maintenance.
20. Starboard platform airlock.
21. Inspection platform.
22. Thunderbird 3 docking ring position clamp.

Docking arm antennae: the twin-gate scanners on the docking arm provide meteor detection and space communication scanning capability.

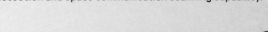

SECONDARY VEHICLES

The key to the success of many International Rescue missions can be attributed to the effective use of specialised rescue vehicles capable of carrying out otherwise impossible tasks. These vehicles have been designed for maximum efficiency and versatility, and to be suitable for use in a wide variety of inhospitable environments.

To enable the best use of resources to be made many of these vehicles are based on commercially available running gear and components, which have usually been completely overhauled and subjected to arduous testing before being approved for use. In many cases power units have been upgraded from standard or replaced with superior alternatives. A programme of development to expand and improve the existing range is constantly ongoing, with the facilities on Tracy Island providing a testing and construction base for new and ingenious machines and equipment.

At times there is no substitute for a practical field trial, however, and covert methods are often

Secondary vehicles

employed to test new design developments. The recent conversion of a UMC Lightning sports car and its entry into a Grand Prix race has provided one way to trial a new turbine unit and drivetrain. Geographical surveys and field trials in remote areas also prove vital in developing environmentally adaptable equipment, and to allow on-site research to be carried out a fully equipped caravan train is available for extended expeditionary ventures.

In addition to the vehicles and equipment used specifically for International Rescue purposes, facilities on Tracy Island also house a number of household aircraft and seagoing craft, including Jeff Tracy's personally designed supersonic jet and Tin-Tin's self-modified Ladybird aircraft. In contrast to the advanced technology normally used by the Tracy family, the latest vehicle to find a home on the island is a vintage Tiger Moth bi-plane, currently undergoing a nut-and-bolt restoration by Alan Tracy (with some assistance from Tin-Tin!). A far cry from the rugged and technologically sophisticated rescue vehicles designed by Brains, a less likely addition to the International Rescue fleet would be hard to imagine.

MOLE

An immensely powerful tunnelling machine, the Mole is capable of drilling through the hardest rock and man made material thanks to a drill bit formed from the Cahelium derived alloy Formula C30/1. With the aid of a three dimensional thermal imaging system, the Mole can pinpoint the position of any trapped individuals with precise accuracy. Caterpillar tracks built into each side of the tunneller unit enable it to reverse to the surface and re-engage with the cradle on its tracked trolley.

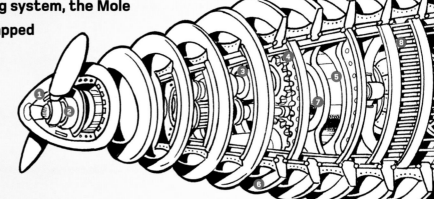

Mole

1. Drill bit, constructed like the main drill from cahelium with Formula C30/1 additives.
2. Acoustic detector and 3D thermal imaging system scans the ground ahead of the Mole during tunnelling operations. Positions of victims are logged on the Mole's computer system and the data is transferred instantly to Thunderbird 2. Laser cutters or smaller hand-held drilling equipment can then be deployed for more delicate operations.
3. Multiple bearing system with main drive sprocket ring turns drill bit independently of outer drill casing.
4. Drive sprocket ring.
5. Electric generator.
6. Revolving outer drill casing, constructed from cahelium with Formula C30/1 additives.
7. Electric motor drives sprocket rings via a multiple gearing system, powered by adjacent reactor.
8. Annular bearing rings.

9. Shielded nuclear fusion reactor provides power to electric generators operating the drill, caterpillar tracks, rear thruster and life-support.
10. Main control console operates Mole trolley and doubles as a mobile rescue control unit.
11. Operator's seat.
12. Bench seating can be folded down to provide bunk space, room for stretchers or storage for hover-jets.
13. Pressure and temperature sensors.
14. Warning light, used before drilling commences.
15. Top-side exit hatch.
16. Rear thruster motor provides additional thrust when drilling.
17. Storage bay contains: hand-held rescue equipment, medical supplies and thermal suits.
18. Mole diagnostic display monitor.
19. Air tanks.
20. Port side caterpillar track provides additional traction when drilling and allows the Mole to reverse direction of travel if necessary.
21. Port side caterpillar sprocket drive.

22. Caterpillar drive electric motor.
23. Life-support monitoring controls.
24. Air-recycling and life-support systems.
25. Liquid oxygen tanks, used as an oxydant with rocket fuel propellant.
26. Fuel pump.
27. Brake, clutch and gearing systems.
28. Trolley fuel propellant tanks.
29. Port side trolley engine turbine.
30. Port side exit hatch.
31. Hydraulic jack lifts upper section of trolley to desired drilling angle.
32. Air intakes.
33. 1000bhp high-compression engine powering twin turbines, using rocket propellant with air or, in some circumstances, liquid oxygen as an oxidant.
34. Demolition missile battery can be used to remove surface obstacles prior to drilling if no victims are located in drilling area.

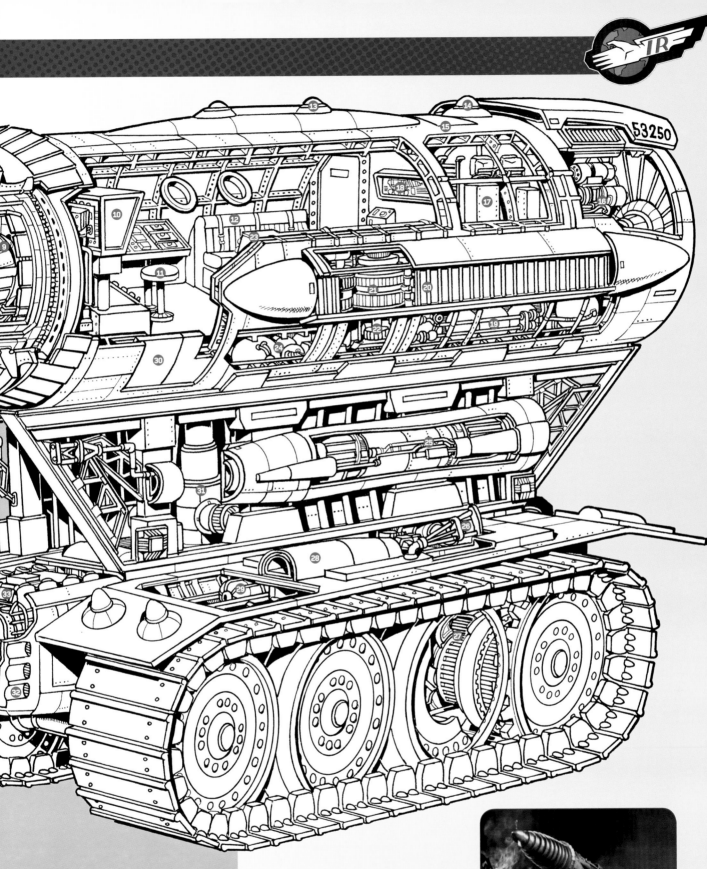

53250

35 Thermal imaging camera locates victims near the surface of the proposed drilling area prior to rescue operations.

Guidance sensors: the Mole is guided by forward-mounted sensors to the optimum drilling point.

A dual-purpose fire-fighting and debris-clearance vehicle, the Firefly's forward-mounted shield is constructed of Cahelium Extract-X providing heat protection from intense temperatures and resilient dozer blade capability. The shield allows access for the barrel of a heavy-duty gun armed with nitro-glycerine shells. These can be used to snuff out otherwise uncontrollable fires and for major debris clearance. Rear-mounted water and foam dispensers can be used for vehicle cooling purposes and for blaze control.

Firefly

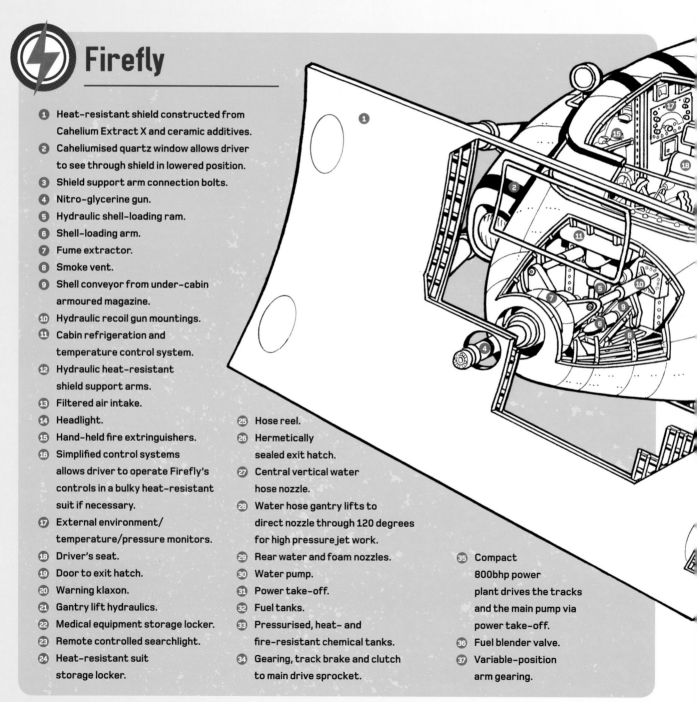

1. Heat-resistant shield constructed from Cahelium Extract X and ceramic additives.
2. Caheliumised quartz window allows driver to see through shield in lowered position.
3. Shield support arm connection bolts.
4. Nitro-glycerine gun.
5. Hydraulic shell-loading ram.
6. Shell-loading arm.
7. Fume extractor.
8. Smoke vent.
9. Shell conveyor from under-cabin armoured magazine.
10. Hydraulic recoil gun mountings.
11. Cabin refrigeration and temperature control system.
12. Hydraulic heat-resistant shield support arms.
13. Filtered air intake.
14. Headlight.
15. Hand-held fire extinguishers.
16. Simplified control systems allows driver to operate Firefly's controls in a bulky heat-resistant suit if necessary.
17. External environment/temperature/pressure monitors.
18. Driver's seat.
19. Door to exit hatch.
20. Warning klaxon.
21. Gantry lift hydraulics.
22. Medical equipment storage locker.
23. Remote controlled searchlight.
24. Heat-resistant suit storage locker.
25. Hose reel.
26. Hermetically sealed exit hatch.
27. Central vertical water hose nozzle.
28. Water hose gantry lifts to direct nozzle through 120 degrees for high pressure jet work.
29. Rear water and foam nozzles.
30. Water pump.
31. Power take-off.
32. Fuel tanks.
33. Pressurised, heat- and fire-resistant chemical tanks.
34. Gearing, track brake and clutch to main drive sprocket.
35. Compact 800bhp power plant drives the tracks and the main pump via power take-off.
36. Fuel blender valve.
37. Variable-position arm gearing.

Heat Resistance: Firefly's construction allows it to operate in the heart of fire-ravaged areas.

Nitro-Gun: Nitro-glycerine shells can be fired to extinguish flame-outs or clear debris.

ELEVATOR CAR

The high-speed elevator cars have been developed to provide aircraft suffering from undercarriage failure the means of effecting a safe and controlled landing using a conventional airport runway. Up to three remote-controlled cars operated by a manned master vehicle can be pre-programmed into a moving formation to create a cushioned mobile platform configured by a target aircraft's airframe specifications through the use of a car-to-car infrared beam positioning system. Additional guidance fine-tuning can be carried out while the formation is in motion by the controller of the master car. Each car is based on an articulated chassis with high velocity diesel electric motors powering the forward and rear units. Capable of accelerating to a top speed of 180mph within 30 seconds, each car is fitted with high density Plasma-Mould tyres.

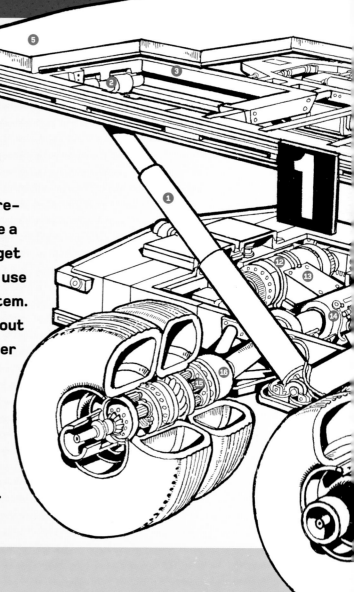

Elevator Car

1. Variable position hydraulic platform support stanchion provides high-impact shock absorbers able to support the weight of most aircraft or heavy loads where appropriate.
2. Platform height adjustment and shock absorbing bearings.
3. Platform stabilisation underside groove into which the hydraulic support stanchion height adjustment bearings are incorporated.
4. Platform height adjustment power unit.
5. Fireproof rescue platform.
6. Primary load-bearing telescopic support column.
7. Hydraulic fluid distribution and management systems.
8. Hydraulic fluid reservoir.
9. Flexible hydraulic fluid distribution feed pipes.
10. Fuel tanks serving front and rear diesel engines.
11. Fuel pump and distribution valves.
12. Rotary diesel cylinder engine.
13. Drive transfer box.
14. Rear gearbox.
15. Clutch and brake drums.
16. Universally jointed drive shaft.
17. Front gearbox.
18. Hydraulic suspension.
19. Right-hand air intake.
20. Inner cabin door.
21. Outer access hatch to cabin.
22. Driver's seat.
23. Ergonomically simplified control console allows driver to manually operate and monitor up to three Elevator Cars at once using the steering wheels, foot pedals and voice commands.
24. Master Elevator Car foot pedals control all steering functions.

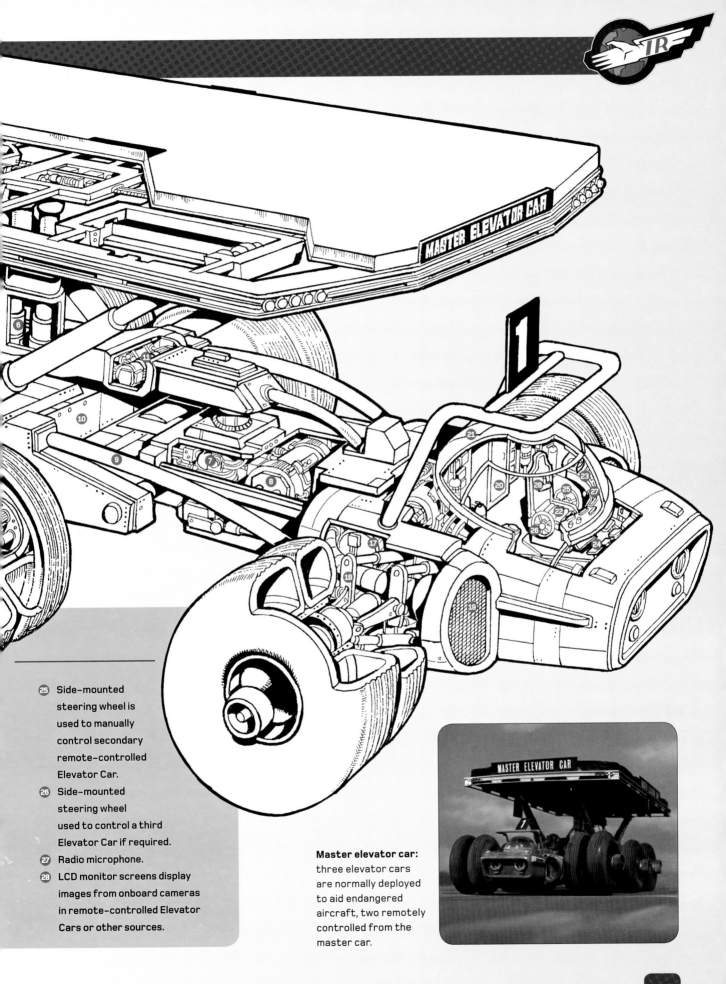

MASTER ELEVATOR CAR

1

25 Side-mounted steering wheel is used to manually control secondary remote-controlled Elevator Car.

26 Side-mounted steering wheel used to control a third Elevator Car if required.

27 Radio microphone.

28 LCD monitor screens display images from onboard cameras in remote-controlled Elevator Cars or other sources.

Master elevator car: three elevator cars are normally deployed to aid endangered aircraft, two remotely controlled from the master car.

RECOVERY VEHICLE

A master recovery vehicle and remote subsidiary can be co-ordinated as a pair to fire clamp-tipped lances connected to 800-foot hawsers at an imperilled vehicle or hazardous structure in order to drag it from a dangerous position. The clamps are launched by powerful compressed-air cannons and can be operated in anti-gravity field, vacuum or electro magnetic mode, and each is capable of hauling weights up to 75 tons.

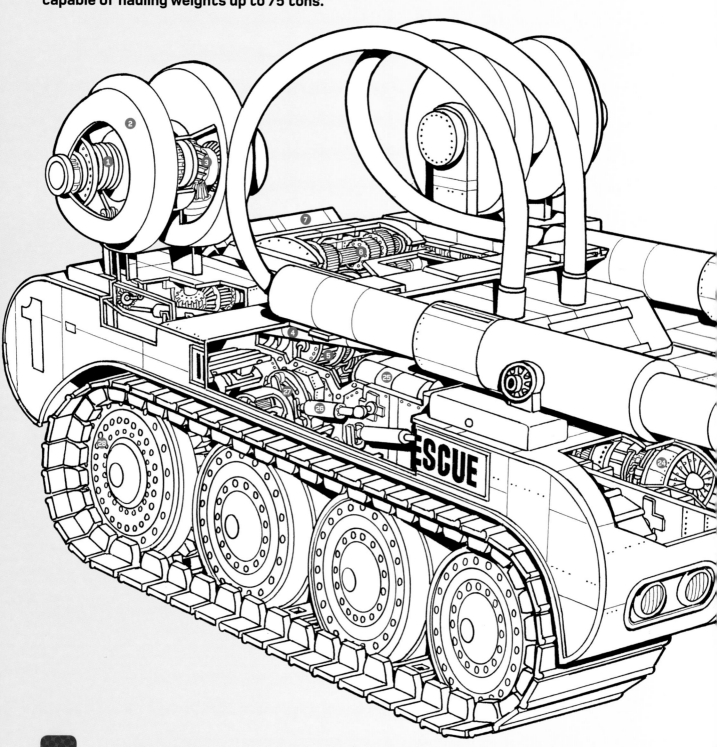

⚡ Recovery Vehicle

1. Cable drum.
2. Fixed cable drum housing.
3. Drum rotation gearing.
4. Starboard cable conduit links cannon to cable storage drum.
5. Cable retraction electric motor.
6. Cable retraction gearing enables the cable to be deployed or retracted at precise speeds to any length required. The system enables the cable to be locked so that the entire vehicle can be used to pull back the rescue target.
7. Motor access panel.
8. Cahelium-strengthened hawser cable.
9. Variable-angle suction clamp cannon hinge.
10. Port suction clamp cannon.
11. Gravity field generator ring.
12. Air/vacuum suction motor.
13. Suction clamps are a combination of artificial gravity generators, vacuum suction and electro-magnetics to provide strong adhesion.
14. Adjustable gravity field projectors.
15. Vacuum suction nozzle.
16. Electro-magnetic rim plate.
17. Hawser triangulation sensor calculates the distance between the vehicle and target to enable the optimum length of cable to be used in a recovery operation.
18. Cahelium-strengthened quartz windscreen.
19. Exit hatch.
20. Communications antenna.
21. Antenna relaying command data from Recovery Vehicle 1 to the remote contolled vehicles.
22. Recovery vehicle systems computer, controlling life support, engine monitoring, suction clamp gravity, suction and electro-magnetics. It also assists the driver to operate the other remote control Recovery Vehicles, and can itself be controlled from TB2 if the driver needs to be elsewhere.
23. Filtered turbine air intake.
24. 900bhp power turbine.
25. Fuel cells.
26. Hydraulic suspension.
27. Gearing, brake and clutch systems.
28. Starboard caterpillar track main drive wheel.

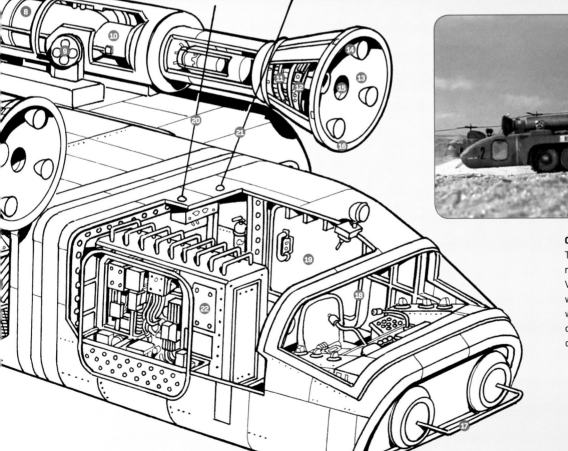

Computer positioning: The master and remote Recovery Vehicles can be guided with exact precision with the aid of a computer controlled operating system.

TRANSMITTER TRUCK

Based on the commercially available Scarab Tractor-cat chassis and designated I.R.3, the Transmitter Truck serves as a mobile platform for a modified Jodrell 6 dish transmitter. The dish can pulse control code signals through space to override internal spacecraft operating systems. A similar beam transmitter unit is built into Thunderbird 3 but has a more limited range.

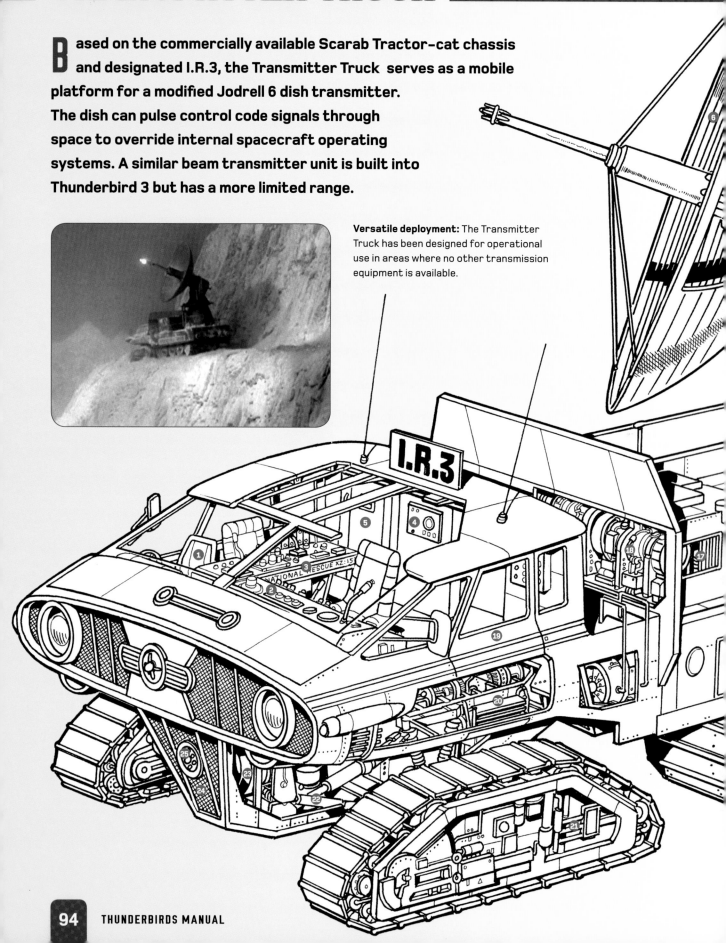

Versatile deployment: The Transmitter Truck has been designed for operational use in areas where no other transmission equipment is available.

I.R.3

⚡ Transmitter Truck

1. Driver's position.
2. Control console operates the truck's dual power systems, external sensors and internal environment systems, plus standard communications.
3. Computerised transmitter dish data analysis and control console.
4. Pressurised cabin enables the truck to be operated in extreme conditions such as mountainous areas.
5. Cabin access to generator housing.
6. Jodrell Six multi-use antenna dish.
7. Data amplification booster.
8. Data processing unit.
9. Antenna dish support stanchions.
10. Turntable.
11. Counterweight grip tracks.
12. Transmitter dish counterweight.
13. Counterweight grip locking jacks.
14. Dish motor control conduits.
15. Fuel tank.
16. Rear caterpillar left-hand clutch and brake system.
17. Generator housing cooling vent.
18. Independent dish power systems.
19. Pressurised cabin door.
20. Retracted cabin access ladder.
21. Forward caterpillar brake and clutch systems.
22. Forward caterpillar track steering arms.
23. Forward caterpillar section power turbine.
24. Forward power turbine air intake.
25. Ground conditions analysis sensors.

INTERNATIONAL RESCUE

I.R.3.

A dual-function rock and debris clearance unit adapted form a Scarab Armadillo utility tractor, adjustable rotating crushers enable the Excavator to clear a path through collapsed rock and other rubble. Powdered residue is jettisoned by powerful extractors to the rear of the machine forming a smooth path for other vehicles. A secondary drill unit mounted centrally can be engaged to create bore holes in solid matter.

Excavator

1. Cabin air supply tank housing.
2. Filtered engine exhaust nozzles.
3. External environment sensor.
4. Warning light array.
5. Left-hand cabin storage bay.
6. Searchlight.
7. Airtight exit hatch.
8. Environmental monitor provides data on atmosphere composition and dust levels from external sensors.
9. Rock crusher controls.
10. Hermetically sealed cabin life-support system monitor and control console.
11. Central data processing computer.
12. Rock cutter and vehicle control consoles.
13. Vehicle steering column.
14. Rock cutter height control link arm with integral power conduit controls the speed and angle of the rotary cutters.
15. Crushed rock rear extraction nozzle.
16. Rear crushed rock duct leading to twin extraction nozzles.
17. Brake and clutch gearing system.
18. Hydraulic suspension.
19. Fuel tanks.
20. 800bhp high-compression engine.
21. Cutter support ram bracing stanchion.
22. Right-hand cutter height adjustment hydraulic ram.
23. Left-hand suction turbine.
24. Filters prevent rock particles from damaging suction turbines.
25. Central duct through which crushed rock and dust is passed to the rear extraction nozzles.
26. Crushed rock collection scoop.
27. Hydraulic rock cutter support beams.
28. Rock cutter armoured power conduits.
29. High-powered primary rotary rock cutters, shown in raised position to allow the precision drill to be deployed.
30. Sealed dust-proof electric drill motor.

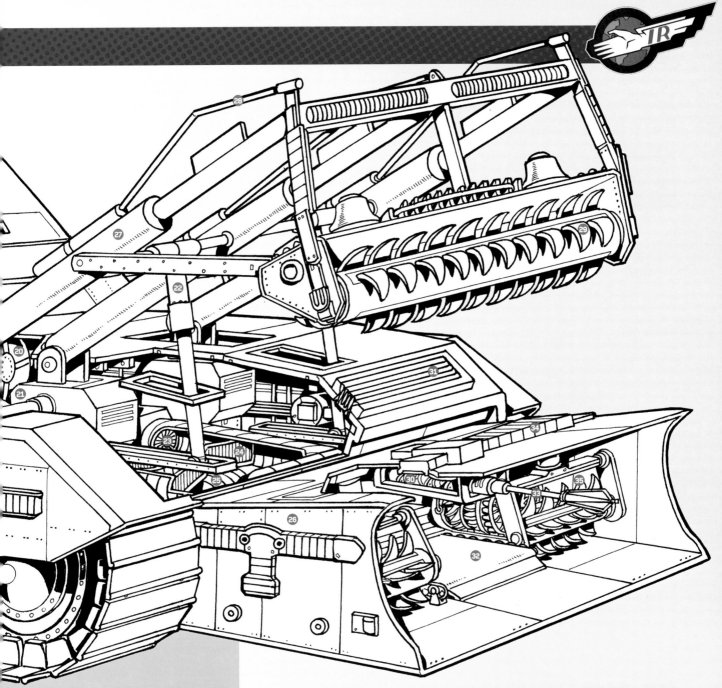

31 Forward sensor array supplies data on the terrain ahead of the vehicle to the central computer in the cabin.

32 Crushed rock conveyor.

33 Precision drill, constructed from Formula C30/1 Cahelium alloy also used on the Mole to drill through the hardest of metals and rock.

34 Magnetic clamp connects the scoop to the primary rotary rock cutter while the vehicle approaches the rescue site.

35 Rock crushers.

Debris disposal: Crushed debris is jettisoned from the rear of the Excavator creating a compacted surface layer.

Secondary drill function: The Excavator is fitted with a powerful drill unit that can cut into the hardest rock strata.

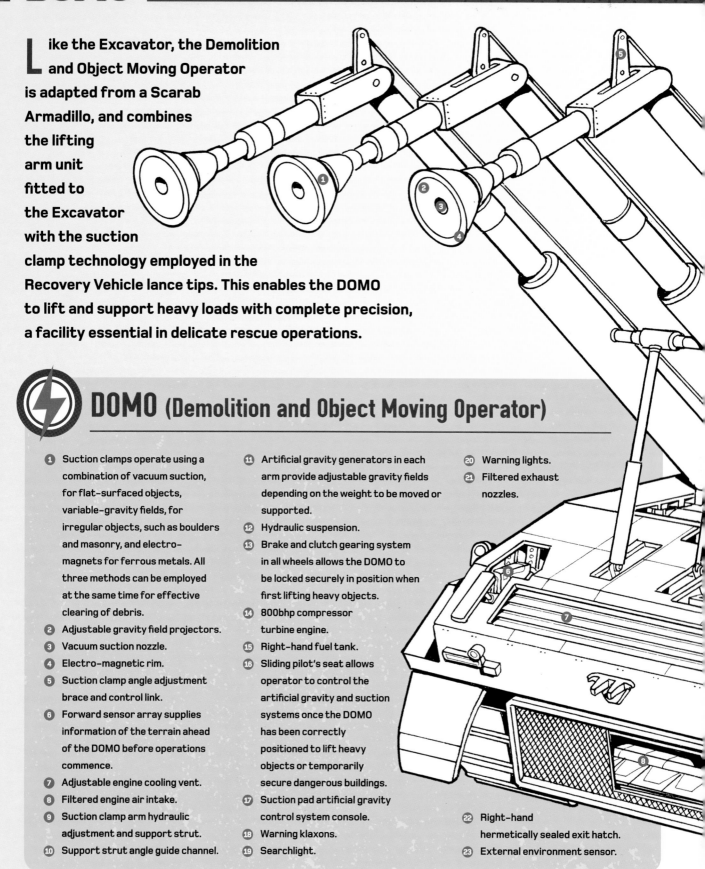

L ike the Excavator, the Demolition and Object Moving Operator is adapted from a Scarab Armadillo, and combines the lifting arm unit fitted to the Excavator with the suction clamp technology employed in the Recovery Vehicle lance tips. This enables the DOMO to lift and support heavy loads with complete precision, a facility essential in delicate rescue operations.

DOMO (Demolition and Object Moving Operator)

1 Suction clamps operate using a combination of vacuum suction, for flat-surfaced objects, variable-gravity fields, for irregular objects, such as boulders and masonry, and electro-magnets for ferrous metals. All three methods can be employed at the same time for effective clearing of debris.

2 Adjustable gravity field projectors.

3 Vacuum suction nozzle.

4 Electro-magnetic rim.

5 Suction clamp angle adjustment brace and control link.

6 Forward sensor array supplies information of the terrain ahead of the DOMO before operations commence.

7 Adjustable engine cooling vent.

8 Filtered engine air intake.

9 Suction clamp arm hydraulic adjustment and support strut.

10 Support strut angle guide channel.

11 Artificial gravity generators in each arm provide adjustable gravity fields depending on the weight to be moved or supported.

12 Hydraulic suspension.

13 Brake and clutch gearing system in all wheels allows the DOMO to be locked securely in position when first lifting heavy objects.

14 800bhp compressor turbine engine.

15 Right-hand fuel tank.

16 Sliding pilot's seat allows operator to control the artificial gravity and suction systems once the DOMO has been correctly positioned to lift heavy objects or temporarily secure dangerous buildings.

17 Suction pad artificial gravity control system console.

18 Warning klaxons.

19 Searchlight.

20 Warning lights.

21 Filtered exhaust nozzles.

22 Right-hand hermetically sealed exit hatch.

23 External environment sensor.

Dual function:
innovative multi-purpose technology allows the DOMO to support and lift immense weights with its telescopic triple arm unit.

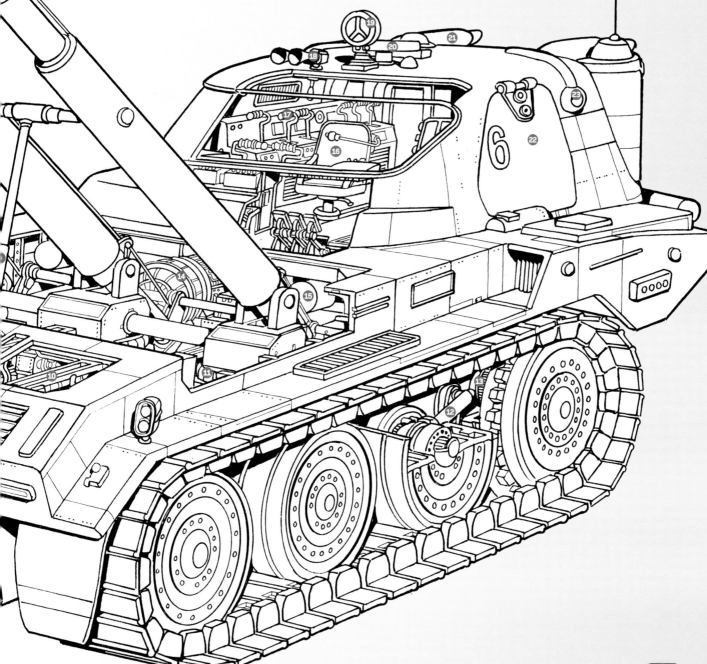

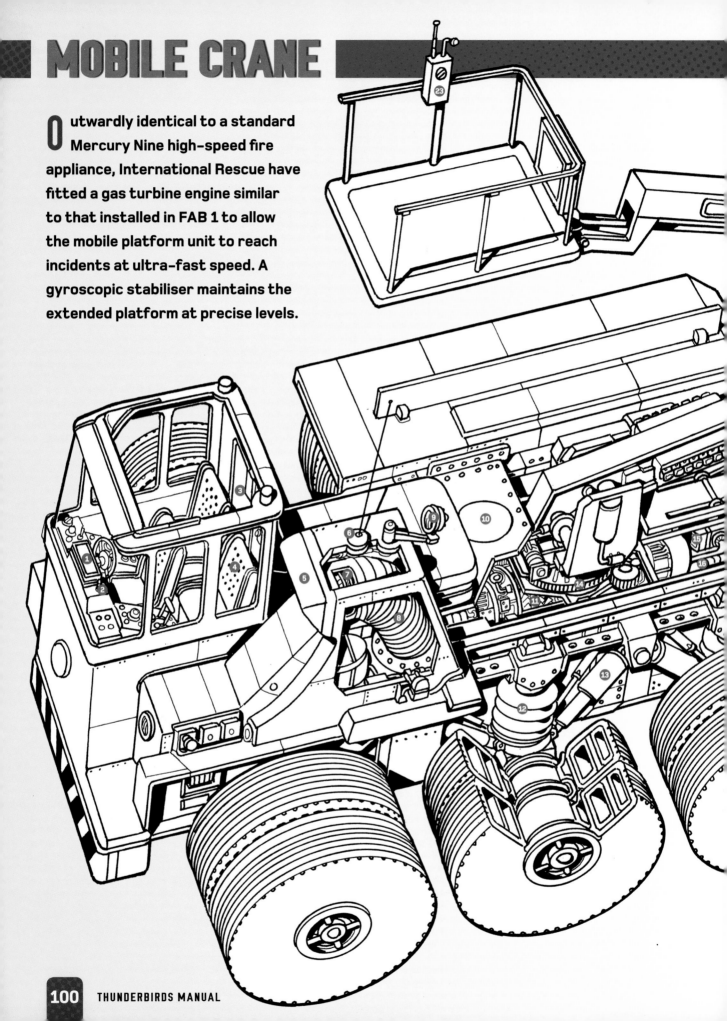

MOBILE CRANE

Outwardly identical to a standard Mercury Nine high-speed fire appliance, International Rescue have fitted a gas turbine engine similar to that installed in FAB 1 to allow the mobile platform unit to reach incidents at ultra-fast speed. A gyroscopic stabiliser maintains the extended platform at precise levels.

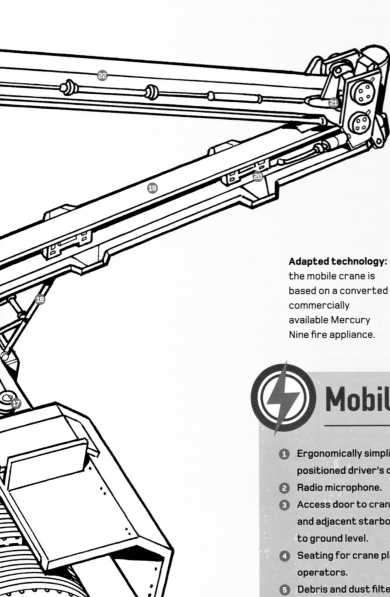

Adapted technology: the mobile crane is based on a converted commercially available Mercury Nine fire appliance.

Mobile Crane

1. Ergonomically simplified, centrally positioned driver's console.
2. Radio microphone.
3. Access door to crane platform and adjacent starboard steps to ground level.
4. Seating for crane platform operators.
5. Debris and dust filter grille for air intake.
6. Communications antenna.
7. Forward air intake fan serving gas turbine air duct.
8. Turbine air duct.
9. Searchlight.
10. Turntable and crane hydraulics cover plate.
11. 500bhp compressor turbine.
12. Shock absorber.
13. Hydraulic suspension.
14. Crane turntable.
15. Gas turbine fuel cell.
16. Exhaust ducts.
17. Exhaust outlet filters.
18. Lower crane beam support locks the crane in position when the vehicle is moving, or when the upper crane beam is in use.
19. Crane beams can raise to up to 90 degrees while keeping the platform horizontal.
20. Lower crane beam.
21. Lockable hydraulic beam pivot.
22. Upper crane beam.
23. Platform height adjustment control box and communications transceiver.
24. Computerised platform auto-level control system ensures that the platform remains horizontal at all times.

MONOBRAKE

The Monobrake allows International Rescue personnel to reach monotrain related incidents by means of an elevating-telescopic-arm-mounted runner adaptable to fit standard- or narrow-gauge monorails. Once clamped in position on the rail, the tracked support unit can be lifted from the ground and propelled forward at speed by jet turbines.

Searchlights: the Monobrake is fitted with two fixed and two adjustable Zenohalogen searchlights providing near daylight-level illumination in sub-surface track-ways.

⚡ Monobrake

1. High-intensity variable power arc lamps, used at night or in tunnels.
2. Standard operating headlights.
3. Steering linkages.
4. Vehicle operator's door.
5. Caterpillar drive power coupling.
6. Brake and clutch gearing systems.
7. Hydraulic suspension and shock absorbers.
8. Fuel tank.
9. Fuel tank valves and regulators.
10. Fuel feed pipes.
11. Jet engine afterburner.
12. Air intake.
13. Turbojet engine.
14. Primary power turbine supplying energy to monorail drive nacelle and forward thrust jet engine.
15. Safety hood protects operator(s) against excess heat from power turbine and jet engine.
16. Turbine supplies power for catapillar tracks.
17. Monorail drive nacelle. When in use the nacelle flips over to clip on to the underside of the monorail. Stability is maintained using guide rollers and electro-magnetic forcefields, ensuring a near-frictionless adhesion to the monorail. This results in speeds up to 480kph thanks to the turbojet engine.
18. Cahelium-strengthened cantilevered rail nacelle arm.
19. Monorail arm power unit supplies energy for the monorail drive nacelle electro-magnetic generators.
20. Multi-layered arm support beams.
21. Nacelle arm stabilising ram.
22. Variable-position guide rollers.
23. Forcefield projectors.

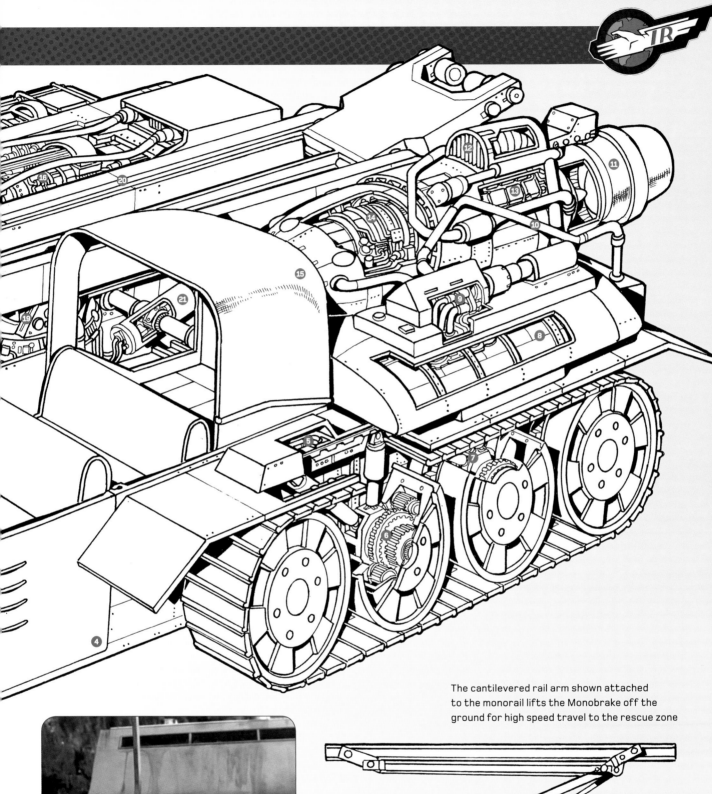

Telescopic runner: once in position beneath a section
of mono-track, the telescopic runner can be attached
to the track and the vehicle propelled by jet engine.

The cantilevered rail arm shown attached
to the monorail lifts the Monobrake off the
ground for high speed travel to the rescue zone

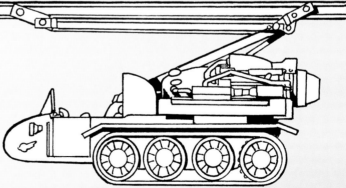

LASER CUTTER AND THUNDERIZER

S everal variations on the Zwerg company's Midget Minidozer have been developed by Brains to assist in a variety of rescue situations. The Laser Cutter projects a high powered beam that can cut through the densest metal with pin-sharp precision, while the Thunderizer is fitted with a powerful projectile cannon that can fire small items at high speed to specific target areas, including capsules containing jet-powered escape harnesses designed to aid those trapped in high buildings.

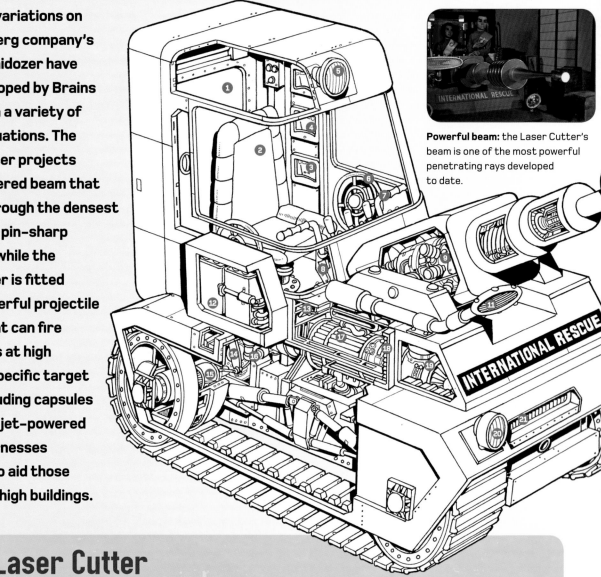

Powerful beam: the Laser Cutter's beam is one of the most powerful penetrating rays developed to date.

⚡ Laser Cutter

1. Access hatch.
2. Driver's seat swivels to allow Laser Cutter operator to access vehicle via rear hatch.
3. External environment sensor monitor.
4. Laser gun diagnostics display.
5. Gun targeting sensor and searchlight.
6. Caterpillar steering controls.
7. Laser gun firing and aiming controls, operated in conjunction with onboard computer.

8. Onboard computer calculates distance, elevation and beam intensity of laser gun.
9. Laser beam generator and power converter.
10. Laser gun radiant cooling vanes.
11. Compressed air jet blaster. Used to blast holes through doors or walls after the laser gun has cut round the area to be accessed.
12. Fuel tanks.
13. Clutch and brake pedals.

14. Clutch and control rods. Steering is achieved by locking the caterpillar tracks on one side enabling the vehicle to 'skid steer'.
15. Right-hand clutch and braking system.
16. Fuel feed valves and conduits.
17. 300bhp high-compression power turbine.
18. Right-hand turbine ventilation/ heat dissipation grille.
19. Turbine compressor turbo fan.
20. Forward headlights.
21. Filtered turbine air intake.

Thunderizer

1. Access hatch.
2. Driver's seat swivels to allow Thunderizer operator to access vehicle via rear hatch.
3. Wind speed and direction monitor.
4. External temperature monitor.
5. External pressure indicator.
6. Searchlight and external environment sensor.
7. Caterpillar steering controls.
8. Mortar firing and aiming controls, operated in conjunction with onboard computer.
9. Onboard computer calculates distance, height and elevation needed to launch each escape harness pod with great accuracy, based on data from pressure, temperature and windspeed sensors.
10. Low-altitude escape harness in mortar auto-loader.
11. One of three escape harness pods, each of which split in two on impact. Inside each pod is a gravity field generator, jet pack and harness allowing the recipient to escape from tall structures.
12. Booster mortar.
13. Fuel tanks.
14. Clutch and brake pedals.
15. Clutch and control rods. Steering is achieved by locking the caterpillar tracks on one side enabling the vehicle to 'skid steer'.
16. Right-hand clutch and braking system.
17. Fuel feed valves and conduits.
18. 300bhp high-compression power turbine.
19. Right-hand turbine ventilation/ heat dissipation grille.
20. Turbine compressor turbo fan.
21. Forward headlights.
22. Filtered turbine air intake.

A further variation on the Zwerg Minidozer, the Dicetylene Cage Transporter enables a subsidiary carriage fitted with chemical foam extinguishers to be lowered into lift shafts of burning buildings, a clamp fitment providing the means to salvage a disabled car beneath it.

Dicetylene foam: a super-retardant compressed compound developed to extinguish the most intense flame, Dicetylene foam has proved invaluable in fire related rescues.

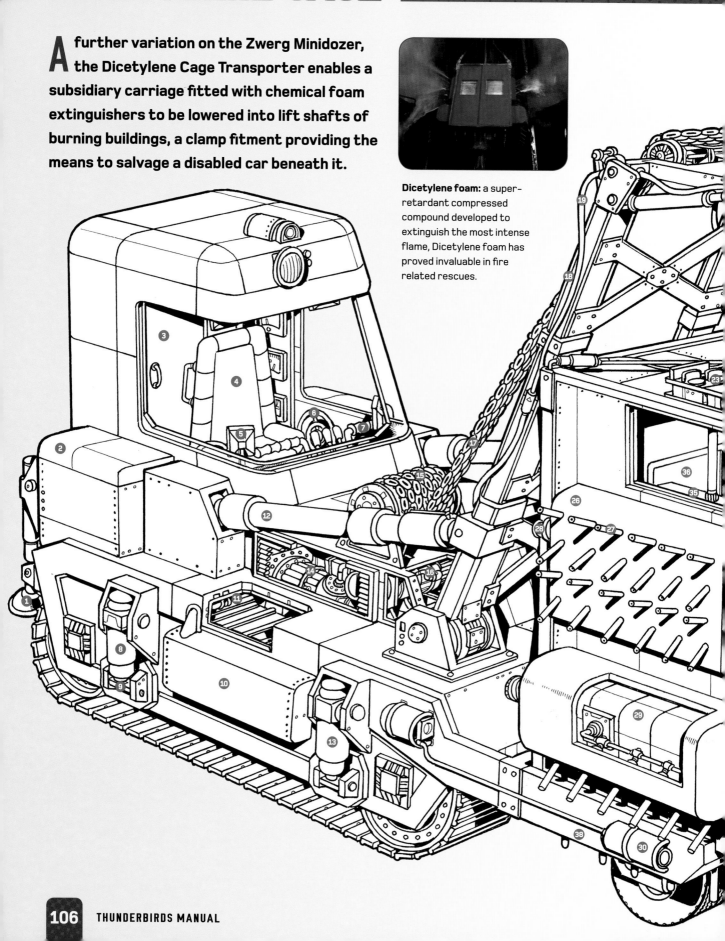

Dicetylene Cage

1. Gravity-assist suction clamp provides additional stability during cage-lifting and lowering operations.
2. Counterweight prevents the vehicle from tipping when cage is deployed. Used in conjunction with suction clamps and stabilisation struts.
3. Rear access hatch to driver's cabin.
4. Driver's seat with handles at rear for an additional cage operator to stand.
5. Video screens relay images to the driver from the front and centrally mounted cameras, providing extra vision when the vehicle is in motion.
6. Caterpillar track steering controls.
7. Cage operating controls.
8. Telescopic clamp support column.
9. Rear right-hand stabilisation strut ensures vehicle does not overbalance when cage is deployed.
10. Right-hand Cahelium-ceramic heat-resistant fuel tank.
11. Fuel feed pipe.
12. Cage support stanchion hydraulic ram.
13. Forward right-hand stabilisation strut.
14. 300bhp high-compression power turbine.
15. Chain drum.
16. Chain drum electric motor.
17. Cahelium-strengthened chains.
18. Telescopic cage support stanchion.
19. Heat-resistant power cable conduit.
20. Lift support head can swivel to allow access to the cage from any direction.
21. Centrally located video camera provides forward vision when the vehicle is in motion and can tilt downwards to monitor the cage's progress during a rescue operation.
22. Lift support head.
23. External environment sensors measure temperature, pressure and atmosphere toxicity.
24. External water supply hose connection valves.
25. Pipes leading to optional external water supply if onboard water tanks run out.
26. Flame-retardant chemical/water tanks.
27. Right-hand multi-directional fire extinguisher nozzles.
28. External water supply valves.
29. Fire-retardant chemical tanks.
30. Right-hand video camera assists driver's forward vision while vehicle is in motion.
31. Lift retrieval hook.
32. Telescopic lift retrieval arm.
33. Water tank.
34. Lift shaft lower level and basement extinguisher nozzles.
35. Life-support systems console and compressed-air tank.
36. Observation window.
37. Communications console.
38. Front-mounted cage support platform with stabilising wheel.

Lowering the cage;
Once in position, the support stanchion extends forward and downwards through hole in wall or lift doorway so that the cage can be lowered.

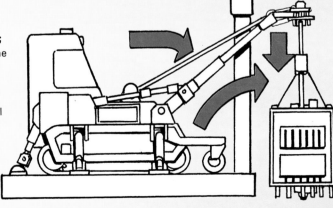

NEUTRALISER TRACTOR

T he Neutraliser Tractor can be deployed to transmit a sonic beam capable of overriding electronic processors built into any device or vehicle.

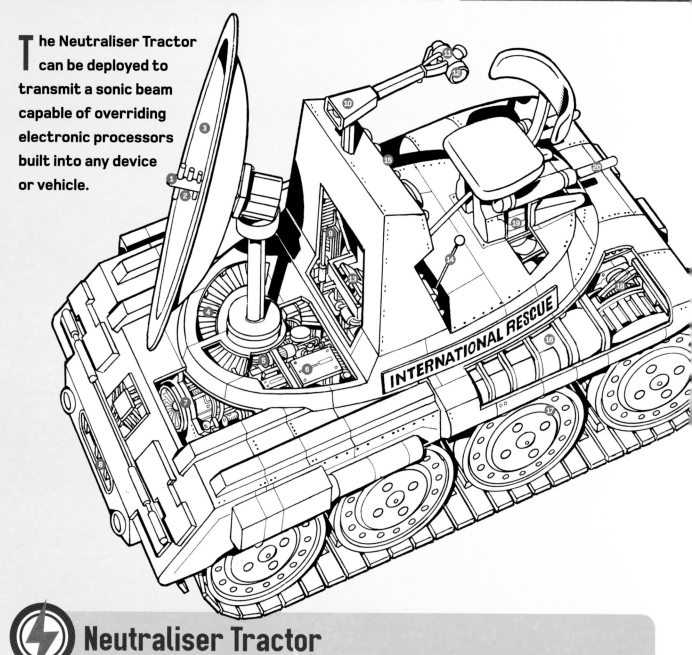

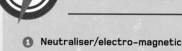

Neutraliser Tractor

1. Neutraliser/electro-magnetic pulse (EMP) beam emitter.
2. EMP emitter focusing receptors.
3. EMP focusing dish.
4. Neutralising/EMP beam generating coils.
5. Beam recharge batteries.
6. Neutralising beam generator power take-off.
7. 200bhp power turbine.
8. Turbine air intake.
9. Onboard computer calculates direction and distance of target, and analyses its construction by matching the components used with electronics information in the database.
10. Computerised target analysis sensor and telescopic rangefinder.
11. Rangefinder eyepiece.
12. Rangefinder adjustment control.
13. Clutch and brake pedals.
14. Neutralising beam activation lever.
15. Neutralising beam controls and driving console.
16. Fuel tanks.
17. Track driving sprocket wheel.
18. Left-hand track clutch and brake drums.
19. Filtered exhaust outlet duct.
20. Exhaust nozzles.

I ncorporating the revolutionary gravity compensation technology under development by Brains, the Jet Air Transporter has been designed to provide a mobile air pressure cushion allowing those trapped in high places to jump safely into a force field shielded column of air.

Jet Air Transporter

1. Forcefield projection array reduces injury to rescue victims floating in the turbofan's updraught. The forcefield is projected upwards and around the craft and its strength can be precisely controlled, allowing victims to be lowered gently onto the vehicle's side-mounted seats, or to the ground if deemed safe to do so.

2. Dual-function variable gravity generator enables the vehicle to hover into the danger area without exerting any downward thrust that might trigger explosive devices. It also generates a forcefield ring using the forcefield projection array.

3. Twin turbofans provide upward thrust for rescues, and rear thrust for propulsion.

4. Air cooling ducts ensure that updraught from the turbofans is prevented from causing burn injuries to rescue victims above them.

5. Forcefield projector.

6. Forcefield intensity field modulator.

7. Gravity lift ring powered by adjacent generator enables vehicle to hover without creating downward thrust.

8. Lift ring electro-magnetic couplings.

9. Propulsion duct pushes vehicle forward. Vanes at the rear outlet force air slightly upward as well as backwards, enabling the vehicle to be propelled forwards.

10. Vertically mounted vanes provide steering.

11. Horizontal vane pushes air away from ground to minimise any detonation risk.

12. Side-mounted seating.

13. Generator fuel cell.

14. Vehicle movement monitor ensures that any air movement caused does not exceed safety limits pre-set and transmitted from the Neutraliser tractor.

15. Driver's console.

16. Forward turbofan power output control switch.

17. Rear turbofan power output control switch.

18. Forcefield projection array intensity monitor.

19. Forcefield intensity control.

20. Forward turbofan output monitor.

21. Rear turbofan output monitor.

22. Gravity lift ring output monitor.

23. Lift ring controls.

JT1 CONDOR

Jeff Tracy's personally designed delta wing jet, the Condor can carry four passengers at speeds in excess of Mach 3. Powered by Tracy Aerospace turbojets supplemented by tailplane mounted ramjets, The aircraft is also fitted with VTOL ramjets, to enable the craft to land on the rooftop helipad of the Tracy Building, the Tracy Corporation's Kansas City skyrise headquarters.

JT1 Condor

1. Dual-control twin pilot's seating.
2. Passenger seating.
3. Instrument panel shroud.
4. Radar modulating units.

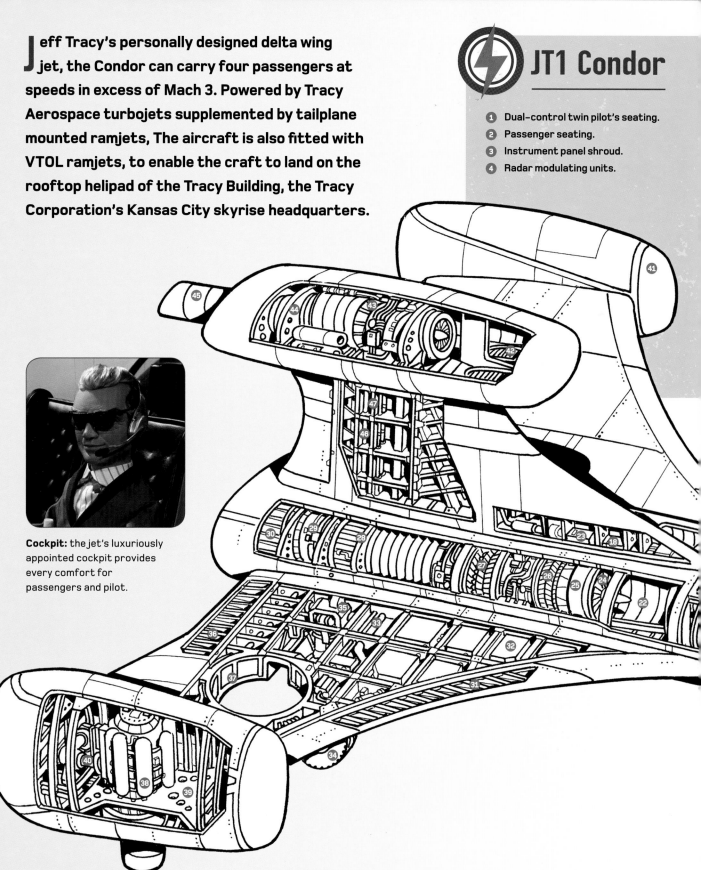

Cockpit: the jet's luxuriously appointed cockpit provides every comfort for passengers and pilot.

5. Scanner dish.
6. Radome.
7. Pitot head.
8. Cockpit pressure floor.
9. Cockpit pressure bulkhead.
10. Nose wheel landing gear hydraulics.
11. Torque scissor links.
12. Nose wheel doors.
13. Nose wheel well.
14. Avionics bay.
15. Luggage compartment.
16. Primary turbine fuel tank.
17. Dual engine fuel tanks serving forward vertical take-off and landing (VTOL) jet and tail-mounted booster jet.
18. Fuel feed pipes and valves from tailplane fuel tank to tail-mounted booster jet.
19. Forward vertical take-off jet.
20. VTOL jet nozzle.
21. VTOL jet cooling vents and primary jet engine air intake.
22. Engine intake centre body.
23. Oil tank.
24. Engine intake compressor face.
25. Forward mounting ring.
26. Tracy aerospace APF12 after-burning turbojet engine.
27. Compressor.
28. Engine rear mounting ring.
29. After-burner nozzle control jacks.
30. Variable-area after-burner exhaust nozzle.
31. Leading edge slat rib construction.
32. Starboard wing fuel tanks serving both rear VTOL jets and main turbojet engine.
33. Fuel pipes and distribution valves.
34. Starboard undercarriage wheel.
35. Undercarriage leg pivot fixing.
36. Aileron rib construction.
37. Rear undercarriage well.
38. Starboard VTOL jet.
39. Jet attachment frame.
40. Fuel feed pipes.
41. Port VTOL jet.
42. Booster jet air intakes.
43. Tail-mounted booster jet.
44. Jet mounting ring.
45. Exhaust nozzle.
46. Tail-mounted engine fuel feed pipes.
47. Reinforced tailplane rib construction.

Delta wing design: designed to Jeff Tracy's own specifications, the Condor is sleek and incredibly fast.

Vertical take-off ramjets: powerful ramjets enable the Condor to lift-off and land without need of a runway.

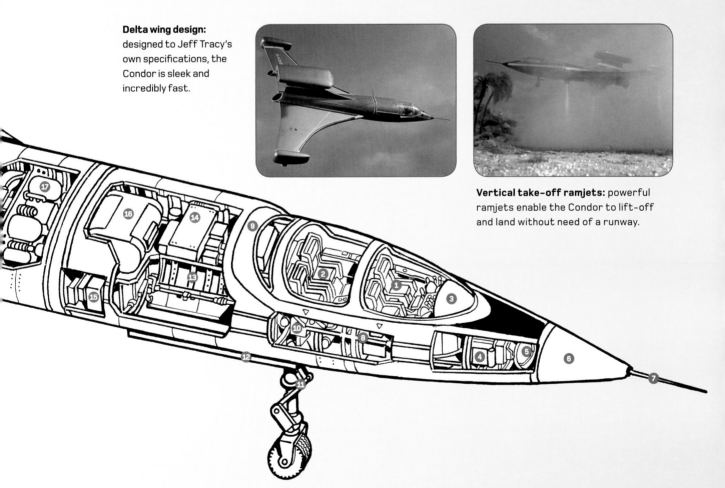

LADYBIRD JET

Developed from a standard Tracy Aerospace supersonic Skylark two seater passenger jet, the Ladybird is Tin-Tin's personal pet project, and has been extensively adapted to her own specifications. Upgraded ramjet boosters and stabilising wingtip fins have improved the aircraft's performance and a lean-burn fuel management system has given increased range. Several of these modifications have now been incorporated into a Skylark carrier based variant, the Seahawk, which is currently under development.

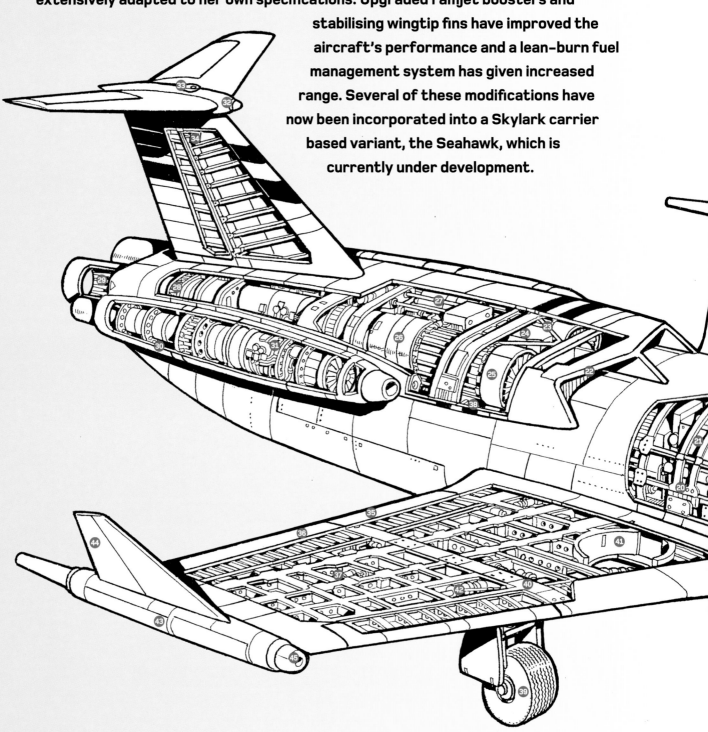

Ladybird Jet

1. Pilot's ejection seat.
2. Passenger's ejection seat.
3. Instrument panel shroud.
4. Radar system module.
5. Scanner tracking mechanism.
6. Radome.
7. Multi-mode radar scanner.
8. Engine throttle levers.
9. Aft-retracting nose wheel.
10. Hydraulic nose wheel steering unit.
11. Torque scissor links.
12. Nose wheel leg door.
13. Retracted cockpit access ladder.
14. Cockpit pressure bulkhead.

15. ADF antenna.
16. Fuselage frame.
17. Avionics bay.
18. VHF antenna.
19. Wing mounting attachment bolts.
20. Wing spar attachment double frame.
21. Fuselage main fuel tanks.
22. Engine bay air intakes.
23. Intake centre body fairing.
24. Oil tank.
25. Main starboard jet engine turbofan.
26. Engine turbine.
27. Control rods.
28. After-burner mounting.
29. Turbojet after-burner nozzle.

30. Starboard ramjet booster unit.
31. Engine hydraulics systems.
32. Tailplane navigation light.
33. UHF antenna.
34. Rudder control linkage actuator.
35. Inner starboard flap.
36. Outer starboard flap.
37. Flap control linkage.
38. Engine mounting trunnion.
39. Starboard main wheel.
40. Undercarriage mounting spar.
41. Undercarriage wheel bay.
42. Undercarriage retraction jack.
43. Wingtip anti-flutter weight.
44. Wingtip stabilising fin.
45. Starboard navigation light.

Personal modifications: the Ladybird Jet has been expertly modified by Tin-Tin, showcasing her engineering skills.

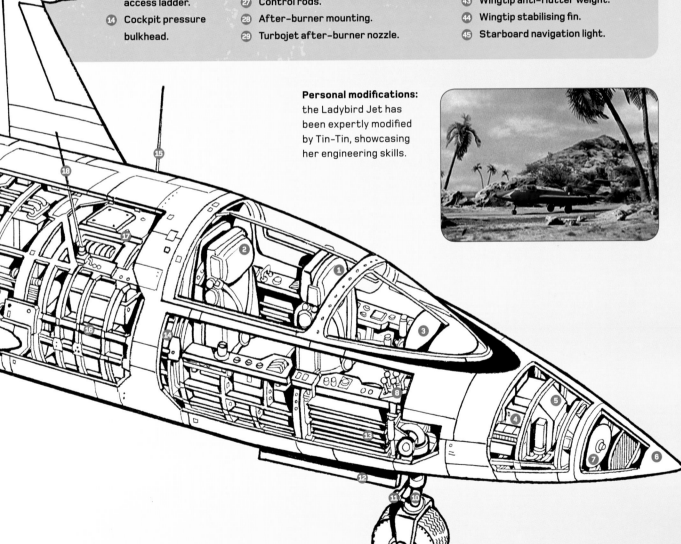

FIELD MISSION HALF-TRACK

A super-tuned version of the standard Global Carrier Cobra All Terrain Vehicle, International Rescue uses the half-track for survey and field testing expeditions in remote areas. Like its sister vehicle, the 12-wheeled Spider, the Cobra is powered by a gas turbine engine, but due to its half-track configuration is considerably slower. On International Rescue field missions the half-track may tow an air-conditioned caravan train, which can accommodate three people and incorporates laboratory and lounge areas.

Multi-terrain vehicle: the Global Carrier Cobra is a well-proven commercial success, providing reliable transportation in extreme environments.

Living accommodation: Air conditioned caravans are available for use by International Rescue team members while on field expeditions.

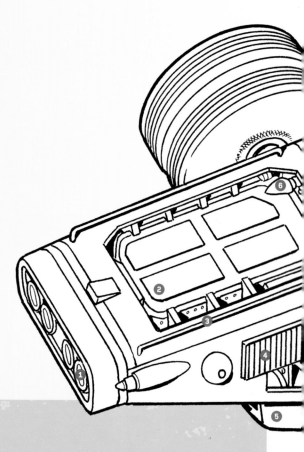

Field Mission Half-track

1. Main headlights.
2. Hydrogen fuel tank.
3. Removable fuel cell cover.
4. Right-hand air intake.
5. Underside filtered engine air intake.
6. Fuel feed regulator valve.
7. Additional fog headlights.
8. Power-assisted steering.
9. Instrument panel.
10. Steering linkage.
11. Refuelling inlet.
12. Turbine air duct.
13. Rear track hydraulic suspension.
14. Starting motor.
15. Fuel pump.
16. Compressor.
17. Combustion chamber.
18. Primary turbine wheel.
19. Secondary turbine wheel.
20. Reduction gearing.
21. Left-hand track clutch and brake drums.
22. Track driving sprocket wheel.
23. Fold-away rear compartment canopy.
24. Removable canopy support rods.
25. Rear storage compartment.
26. Additional side-mounted storage locker with furled spare canopy sheet.

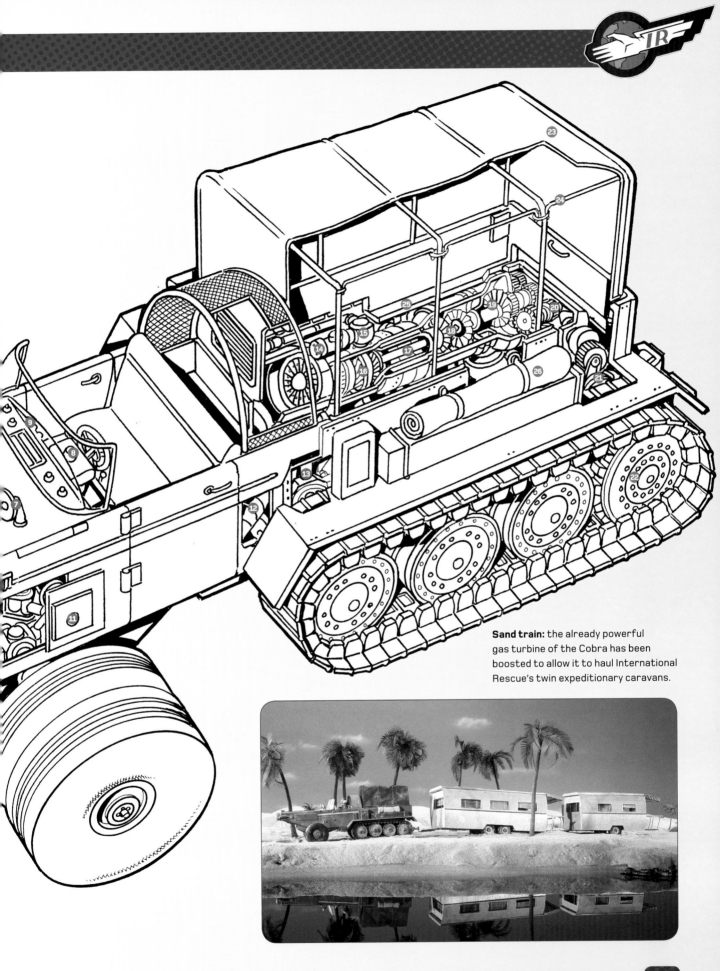

Sand train: the already powerful gas turbine of the Cobra has been boosted to allow it to haul International Rescue's twin expeditionary caravans.

BR2 LIGHTNING 505

D esigned as a mobile test bed for a new generation of lightweight super-efficient gas turbine engines being developed by Brains, the BR2 was the second prototype based on a Universal Motor Company Lightning 505 high-performance racing shell to be engineered in International Rescue's workshop after the BR1 exploded during rolling road trials. Unfortunately the BR2 was also destroyed following its recent participation in the Parola Sands Grand Prix. Brains is now developing the BR3.

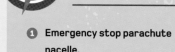

Race Proven: with Alan Tracy at the wheel the BR2 was driven to victory at Parola Sands, demonstrating the power of Brains' new engine.

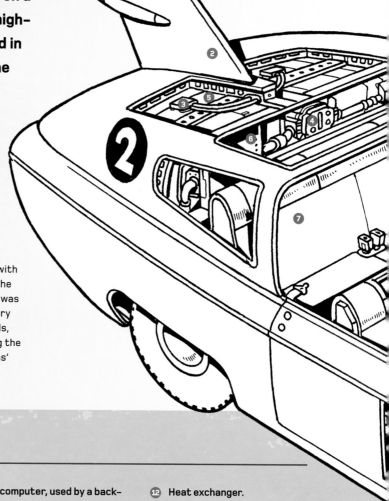

BR2 Lightning 505

① Emergency stop parachute nacelle.

② Tail-fin incorporates antennae maintaining contact with base via TB5.

③ Fuel flow regulators.

④ Fuel pump.

⑤ Starboard hydrogen fuel cell.

⑥ Cahelium-strengthened fuel cell anti-collision bulkhead.

⑦ Rear seats are used by navigator for long-distance rallying and are accessed via the main side doors when the front seat is moved forward.

⑧ Navigation computer, used by a back-seat passenger. Antenna in tail-fin relays information ranging from road and weather conditions from TB5. Also linked to onboard computer monitor display on dashboard.

⑨ One of four headrests, which can be raised hydraulically when the car is being driven at high speeds.

⑩ Vehicle occupant protection forcefield projection array. In the event of a collision, shaped forcefields protect the vehicle's occupants from impact injury.

⑪ Suspension cowling nacelle.

⑫ Heat exchanger.

⑬ Intake cowling.

⑭ Gas turbine intake fan.

⑮ Turbine air intake.

⑯ Combustion chamber.

⑰ Compressor turbine.

⑱ Air cooling duct for front brakes.

⑲ Geared steering linkage.

⑳ Coil-sprung suspension.

㉑ Dashboard-mounted computer and monitor screen operated by driver or front-seat navigator. Displays car's mechanical status and relays data from rear navigation computer.

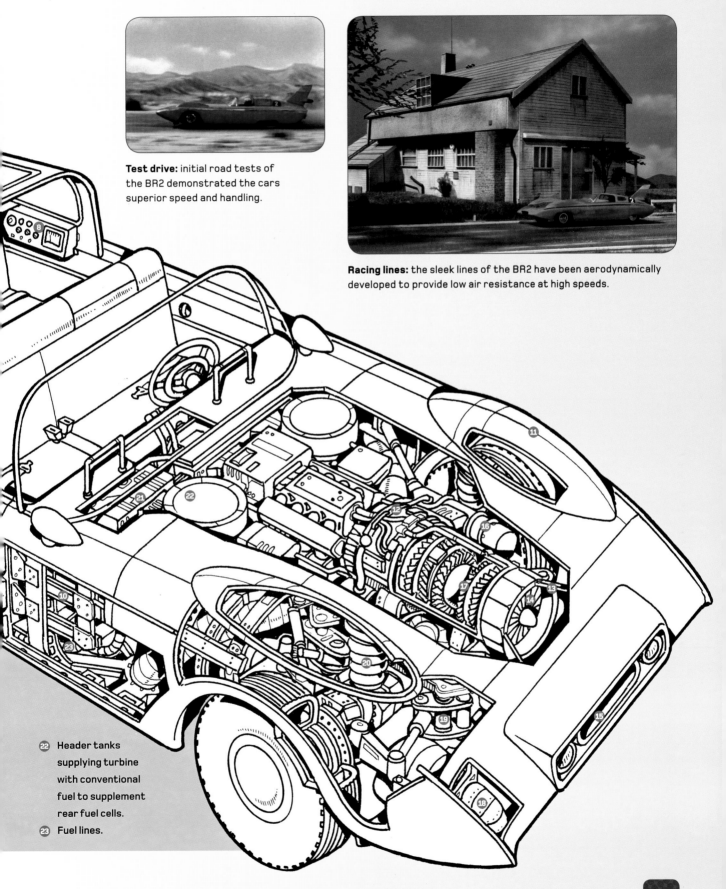

Test drive: initial road tests of the BR2 demonstrated the cars superior speed and handling.

Racing lines: the sleek lines of the BR2 have been aerodynamically developed to provide low air resistance at high speeds.

22 Header tanks supplying turbine with conventional fuel to supplement rear fuel cells.

23 Fuel lines.

GLOBAL OPERATIVES

The successful creation of International Rescue and its continued day to day operation would have been inconceivable without the expert assistance and dedicated support of a global network of agents.

From humble office cleaners and security patrol guards to trans-national company directors and high-ranking military officials, International Rescue can call on an impressive variety of skilled and knowledgeable helpers.

Vital to the supply of components and for the design and manufacture of rescue equipment, the agents are responsible for ensuring the Thunderbirds craft are kept ready for action at

all times, and equipped with the latest devices. A covert courier system supported by access to the services of an international freight corporation allows items and material of any nature to be transported speedily to any destination.

The network also maintains a chain of ground-based communications booster stations. These can be concealed in the most unlikely locations, ranging from an abandoned Siberian salt mine to a dummy office block in Buenos Aires. One of the most important duties of the agents' network is to ensure these stations remain fully operational.

Agents may also be called on at a moment's notice to provide field support during the course of a mission. To aid in their capacity to offer the greatest assistance possible they have been supplied with custom-built devices and communications equipment. From a team of over one hundred agents, a typical representative might be Agent 47 – Jeremiah Tuttle.

Covering the American Midwest, Jeremiah may appear a slow-minded backwoods hillbilly, but appearances could not be more deceptive. A sharp-witted operative with a detailed local knowledge, his homely run-down shack is in fact a highly efficient local monitoring station. An ancient gas cooker conceals a state-of-the-art communications scanner and transceiver, while his dilapidated farm truck can out perform the latest GT sports car,

London Agent
Lady Penelope

AREA OF SPECIALISATION
International Rescue senior troubleshooter, mission support, Agents' network operational advisor.

BACKGROUND
The daughter of Sir Hugh and Lady Amelia Creighton-Ward, Rowden-educated Penelope seemed destined for a life of sheltered privilege. But she soon tired of the superficial high-society world she was born into and sought a more challenging sense of purpose. Through family connections in British Intelligence she began taking on increasingly challenging secret assignments using the cover of a jet-set reporter and international super model. Realising she had acquired a taste for espionage she soon became a fully fledged agent, joining the newly formed Federal Agents' Bureau.

PERSONAL CHARACTERISTICS
Cool and unshakeable, with nerves of finely spun steel, Penelope is completely unflinching in the face of deadly peril, perfectly living up to her personal motto, 'Elegance, Charm and Deadly Danger'.

thanks to the installation of a turbo-boost supercharger. He has even developed his own brand of highly explosive beans. Other agents have been equally appropriately equipped, and none more so than the network's designated agent in chief.

Lady Penelope Creighton-Ward was selected to lead the agents' network on the strength of her experience as an operative for the Federal Agents Bureau, the international espionage agency formed to provide a global security service answerable to the provisional World Government. To the outside world her Ladyship may appear to be a harmless social butterfly, leading a life of frivolous pleasure, but nothing could be further from the truth. The glamorous façade of her aristocratic lifestyle conceals a diamond-sharp determination to carry out the most dangerous assignment to a successful conclusion.

Based in England at her family home in Foxleyheath, Penny, as she prefers to be known, is ready at a moment's notice to jet off on an urgent mission whenever a call comes through on her sterling silver radio transmitter teapot. To aid her in her undercover activities she can call on the invaluable assistance of her reformed ex-convict manservant Parker, and a lethal armoury packed into her exploding handbag or worn as matching accessories. She also carries the latest bugging and anti-bugging devices with her at all times.

To match her deceptively glamorous appearance, the titled troubleshooter also has at her disposal a shocking pink six-wheeled Rolls-Royce, FAB 1, which outwardly betrays no evidence that it is more than a match for the latest hover-tank. A private jet and a personal yacht are also available to provide additional transportation when required. With such technical resources and personal resourcefulness to call on, the International Rescue agents' network is more than a match for any situation.

FAB 1

Beneath its deceptively smooth lines FAB 1 provides International Rescue's London Agent with an impressive range of concealed gadgetry

FAB 1
Technical data

POWER
ENGINES: Modified Rolls–Royce gas turbine Vortex aquajet for water travel

DIMENSIONS
LENGTH: 21 feet
WIDTH: 8 feet
WEIGHT: 3 tons

ARMAMENT
FRONT: 2 machine guns and 1 central machine cannon
REAR: 2 machine guns, 4 harpoon launchers, smokescreen canister, oil slick dispenser and 2 laser guns

PERFORMANCE
LAND SPEED: 200mph+
SEA SPEED: 50 knots

TECHNOLOGY DATA FILE

Custom built for the Creighton-Ward family by the Rolls-Royce company, FAB 1 is powered by one of the firm's most powerful hybrid mini gas turbine power units. To support the weight of the turbine, twin-steering front-wheel assemblies are required, resulting in a unique six-wheeled chassis, the arrangement also giving the double benefit of greater stability when cornering.

Powered at low revolutions by conventional fuel sources, proton-conducting solid-oxide fuel cells can be engaged to boost the turbine's power, enabling a maximum speed in excess of 200mph to be achieved. To complement the vehicle's unique engineering, equally unconventional bodywork was created, sweeping back in an aerodynamically efficient streamlined shape from the traditional Rolls-Royce radiator grille.

To add to the aerodynamic effect and to provide maximum visibility, the passenger compartment is topped by a transparent bubble incorporating opening gull-wing sections. These are combined with retractable lower doors to provide access for passengers. In contrast, the leather and wood trimmed interior is relatively understated, its most unusual feature being the centrally positioned driving seat. This affords the driver unrestricted vision and allows ease of access for passengers to the rear bench seat. For additional rear view vision the driver can switch in cameras mounted in the boot and at either side of the canopy to relay images to the two dashboard display monitors.

Although remaining outwardly unchanged, FAB 1 has been almost entirely rebuilt since it first left the Rolls-Royce factory to cater for its present owner's undercover activities. Initially modified by the Federal Agents Bureau, whose Undercover Weapons and Equipment division fitted numerous gadgets to the vehicle, FAB 1 was again thoroughly reconstructed to specifications devised by Brains in the Tracy Island laboratories.

Beneath its sleek bodywork, FAB 1 now boasts an arsenal of weaponry and an impressive range of high-tech gadgetry. At the touch of a button on the dashboard the driver can engage rear-mounted spears, laser guns, oil slick and smokescreen dispensers, and twin-mounted machine guns. The front of the car is similarly well armed, boasting directional machine guns, which also function as sniper rifles, and a centrally mounted high-powered machine cannon concealed behind the famous radiator grille. Other weaponry and defensive devices include tyre slashers and bullet-proof tyres fitted with retractable studs to aid grip.

Other modifications to the car to increase its versatility and mission practicality include a lift located in the boot, skis and hydrofoils. The car's communications equipment has also been upgraded with Neutroni transceiving components, and infrared and thermal imaging cameras fitted to the front and rear. Most importantly, the body shell, canopy and internal mechanics have been entirely rebuilt with super toughened materials rendering the car virtually indestructible.

Driver
FAB 1
Aloysius Parker

DESIGNATED ROLE
London Agent's General Factotum and Associate Mission Operative.

AREA OF SPECIALISATION
Armoured limousine transport duties, security system immobilisation, underworld community liaison.

BACKGROUND
Born into a long line of family retainers, Aloysius Parker found his employment prospects in service ruined as a result of a family feud. Encouraged by a criminal gang he had fallen in with, he turned his skills at mechanical engineering and thermo-technical dynamics to dishonest use. An extended 'oliday' in Parkmoor Scrubs did not cure his crooked tendencies, and he returned to his life as an expert safe-breaker. His skills brought him to the attention of Lady Penelope who 'encouraged' him to turn his talents to more productive use.

PERSONAL CHARACTERISTICS
A devoted, loyal and trustworthy character, Parker barely raises an eyebrow when asked to take part in another dangerous mission for his employer and can be relied on to retain a sense of humour in the most desperate situation.

FAB 1

One of the most eye-catching cars ever built, FAB 1's gleaming pink exterior conceals an armoury of weapons and a range of sophisticated mechanical and electronic devices. Powered by a compact gas turbine jet engine, the car can reach top speeds in excess of 200mph.

FAB 1 Overview

1. Right-hand wing mirror with integrated video camera.
2. Dashboard-mounted computer and engine diagnostics system.
3. Non-direct steering system computer links steering wheel movements to underside steering linkages via power conduits.
4. Central power steering wheel connected to non-direct driving system computer.
5. Communications microphone.
6. Filtered exhaust outlet.
7. Airbrake power take-off pipe.
8. Power turbine.

Radiator cannon: concealed behind FAB 1's traditional radiator grille, a high powered machine cannon is equipped to fire explosive charges.

9. Combustion chamber.

10. Heat exchanger.

11. Compressor.

12. Gas turbine air intake fan.

13. Moveable radiator grille slats allow machine cannon to be deployed.

14. Directional signal locator processing unit operates via spirit of ecstasy array.

15. Spirit of ecstasy signal locator array.

16. Forward video camera 'sees' through Rolls – Royce badge.

17. Power cells operating vehicle electronics.

18. Centrally positioned machine cannon.

19. Machine cannon projectile cartridge.

20. Storage well doors ensure the machine cannon is protected below the turbofan mounting level when not in use.

21. Machine cannon storage well.

22. Machine cannon deployment hydraulics.

23. Dual-mode indicator/headlight.

24. Left-hand machine gun deployed via open central headlight.

25. Multi-mode indicator/brake light.

26. Central headlight unit swings to one side so that the machine gun can be used.

27. Variable-intensity headlight LED array.

28. Right hand machine gun.

29. Rotary machine gun ammunition cartridge.

30. Forward retracted ski.

31. Hydraulic ski deployment arm.

32. Flexible seals on suspension, steering linkages, ski and hydrofoil deployment arms prevent water flooding the engine when travelling on water.

33. Ski retraction and deployment motor.

34. Emergency airbrake nozzles in retracted position.

35. Watertight bulkhead prevents engine flooding when hydrofoils are in use.

36. Shock absorber.

37. Hydraulic coilsprung suspension.

38. Steering linkages.

39. Vortex aqua jet powered by turbine provides power when FAB 1 uses hydrofoils.

40. Forward retracted hydrofoil.

41. Hydrofoil retraction/deployment motor.

42. Disc brakes.

43. Retracted tyre slasher blade.

44. Retracted studs incorporated into all six bullet-proof tyres, used in snow and icy road conditions.

FAB 1

FAB 1

To enable FAB 1 to meet the widest possible range of mission requirements, the vehicle is fitted with a boot lift, hydrofoils and skis. A vortex turbojet provides forward thrust when the ski or hydrofoil options are selected.

⚡ Equipment

1. Guard rail.
2. Lift platform.
3. Jointed lift platform stabilization hydraulics.
4. Car boot opened clear of platform.
5. Lift-support column.
6. Oil slick spray bar shown in deployed position.
7. Underside ski storage wells.
8. Rear skis are deployed forwards and downwards when required for snow travel.
9. Vortex turbojet provides power for FAB 1 when either the skis or the hydrofoils are deployed. When in use, the turbojet is deployed clear of the heat-resistant underside of the car.
10. Forward hydrofoil shown in partially deployed position. When fully lowered, the blades extend well below the level of the wheels, lifting the car clear of the water.
11. Forward skis shown in deployed position.
12. Skis move down and outwards when deployed for snow travel.

PLATFORM OPERATION

To operate the lift, the boot is opened clear of the lift platform ❶ When not in use, the lift's support column lies flat under the platform. A hydraulic ram pulls the base of the column towards the front of the car ❷ At the same time, the top of the column with the lift platform above raises to 90 degrees ❸ Simultaneously, the guard rails unfold as the operative steps on the platform ❹ The column extends to the required height ❺ The jointed top section of the column ensures the lift platform remains stable ❻

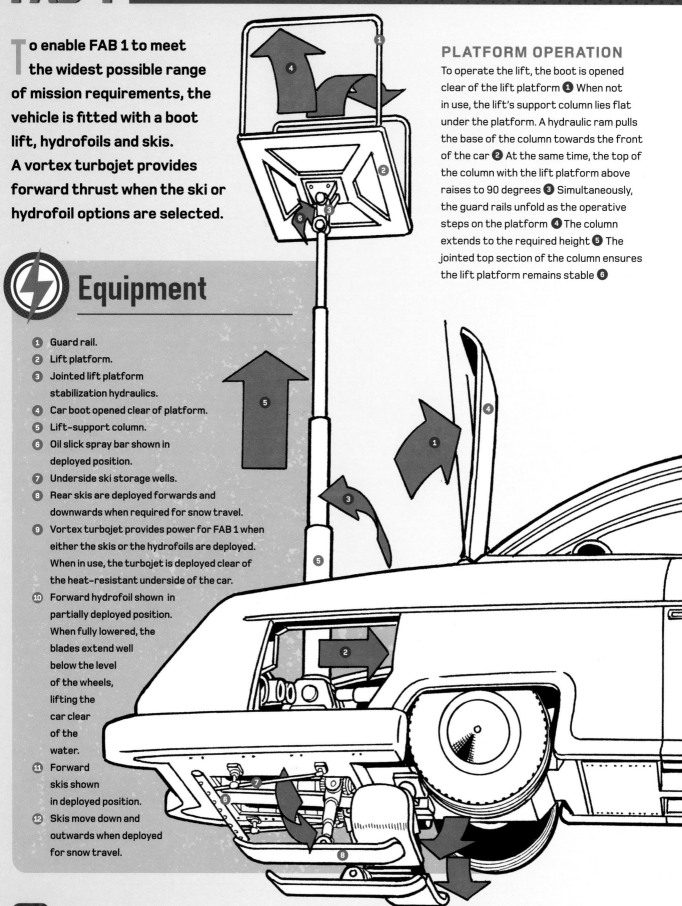

I   Auxiliary traction control panel.

J   Direction indicator and wiper stalk.

K   Speedometer.

L   Function selection indicator on horn button.

M   Turbine thrust indicator.

N   Turbine and vortex jet acceleration and brake pedals.

O   Advance and reverse motion selector stalk.

P   Hydro systems control panel.

Q   Multi-function view-screen.

R   Function control joystick.

S   Forward retro rocket control.

T   Function selection control.

U   Off-side retractable target reticule.

V   Warning lights.

X   Fuel monitor.

Y   Altimeter

Z   Lighting controls.

A   Neutroni transceiver unit.

B   External temperature gauge.

C   Engine systems monitor.

D   Nearside retractable target reticule.

E   Air-conditioning control.

F   Vortex jet control.

G   Multi-function View-screen.

H   Air brake.

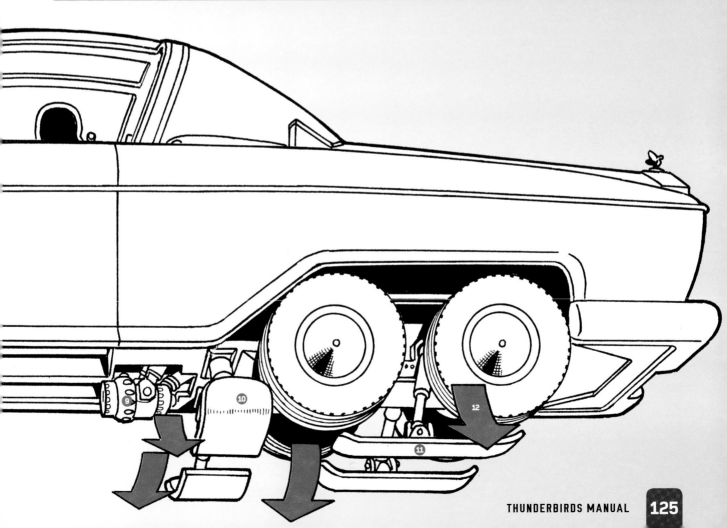

FAB 1

FAB 1's boot boasts a host of specialised extras including twin machine guns, laser cannons and a hydraulic lift. Control of the car is from a centrally positioned driver's seat fitted with a rear-facing viewing screen for passenger use.

Smokescreen: to evade pursuers FAB 1 can release a high-density smokescreen.

Retractable doors: FAB 1 is fitted with a unique retractable door mechanism for ease of access.

Rear compartment

1. Lift guard rails.
2. Lift platform telescopic support column. When deployed, the hydraulic ram pulls the column forward as it tilts to a 90-degree upright position, with the passenger on board. The passenger can raise the guard rails manually as the lift rises, or it can be done automatically if required.
3. Hydraulic ram pulls lift platform column into upright position.
4. Support column base in stowed position.
5. Left-hand harpoon launchers.
6. Harpoon retrieval cable reel.
7. Harpoon cable rewind motor.
8. Machine gun nozzle in extended position.
9. Machine gun ammunition cartridge.
10. Left-hand machine gun.
11. Rear lights shown in retracted position to enable the harpoons, gun or smoke cannister to be used.
12. Cahelium-reinforced inner frame.
13. One of four harpoons (can be used as a weapon without a cable). With cable attached, can be used to pull heavy objects or remove doors.

14. Oil slick bar retraction hydraulics.
15. Underside oil slick spray bar shown in deployed position.
16. Oil reservoir for oil slick system.
17. Oil distribution valve.
18. Left-hand smoke cannister.
19. Right-hand smoke cannister.
20. Right-hand rear machine gun.
21. Right-hand harpoon launchers.
22. Multi-directional laser cannon (shown retracted).
23. Right-hand gas turbine engine fuel cell.
24. Right-hand rear snow ski (shown retracted).
25. Right-hand rear hydrofoil (shown retracted).
26. Laser cannon power unit.
27. Satellite communications and GPS antenna maintains link with TB5 and Tracy Island.
28. Neutroni radio, TV and phone link antenna.
29. Right-hand 'down and under' door.
30. Centrally positioned driver's seat.
31. Computer, video and TV screen, and tracking system monitor.
32. Manually operated machine gun sniper sight and rangefinder.

33. Dashboard GPS, gunsight and tracking systems.
34. Communications microphone.
35. Right-hand wing TV camera.
36. Right-hand 'gull-wing' canopy door.

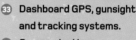

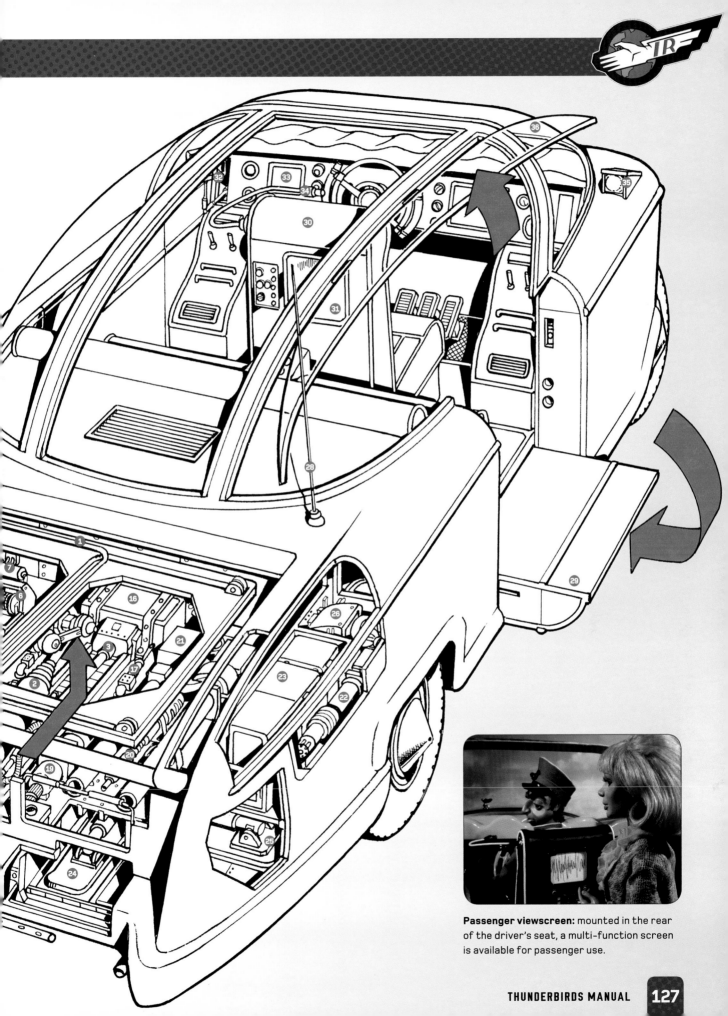

Passenger viewscreen: mounted in the rear of the driver's seat, a multi-function screen is available for passenger use.

ady Penelope's luxury ocean-going yacht is
the latest in a succession of vessels owned
by her Ladyship, its most recent predecessor,
Seabird 1, having been lost at sea following an
attack by a robot mastermind. Like Seabird 1,
FAB 2 has been fitted out to the highest
standard, and apart from lavish accommodation,
including a personal state room for
her Ladyship, the craft also
benefits from the latest
communication and
navigational systems.

FAB 2 Overview

1. Rear-mounted lifeboat.
2. Rear promenade deck.
3. Stateroom en-suite shower facilities.
4. Lady Penelope's stateroom.
5. Inflatable life raft lockers.
6. One of five lifeboats (two on each side and one at the rear) each containing an all-weather canopy, survival kit and built-in GPS system.
7. Upper promenade deck.
8. Washroom located behind navigation bay.
9. Generator cooling vent.
10. Solar energy generator.
11. Radar scanner.
12. Solar panels.
13. Satellite communications array links FAB 2 with Lady Penelope's mansion, Tracy Island or other I.R. Operatives via TB5.

14. Computer and navigation bay.
15. Master stateroom with en-suite facilities reserved for VIP guests.
16. Engineering and yacht systems monitor panel.
17. Starboard promenade deck.
18. Starboard door to dining room.
19. Searchlight.
20. Dining room, occupying the full width of the yacht.
21. Ergonomically simplified control console allows FAB 2 to be controlled by Parker or a single crew member if other crew members are otherwise engaged.
22. Access to dining room, bedrooms and aft decks via starboard promenade deck/corridor.
23. Forward lounge and bar.
24. Door to central corridor.
25. Door to forward central corridor leading to Lill's room, laundry and shower room.

26. Lill's room, if she is accompanying her Ladyship on the yacht.
27. Foredeck storage locker contains emergency equipment.
28. Foredeck access hatch.
29. Air conditioning vent.
30. Forward central corridor.
31. Emergency towing cleat.
32. Shower room.
33. Water purification plant.
34. Sonar system and computerised torpedo guidance system.
35. Retractable sonar array.
36. Air-locked starboard torpedo tubes.
37. Starboard anchor.
38. Lift from galley to bar and dining room.
39. Torpedo auto-loading bay.
40. Laundry.

Guidance System:
FAB 2 can be navigated entirely automatically with the aid of GEORGE (GEO Positioning Remote Guidance Encoder).

41. Galley occupies the full width of the yacht, with access to the central corridor to the rear, and access to Lill's room, laundry, and bathroom to the fore.

42. Underside video cameras encased in cahelium-bonded transparent dome. The twin cameras with powerful lights can be lowered through the keel access hatch to monitor any activity below the vessel.

43. Crew sleeping quarters.

44. Starboard turbine aquajet.

45. Door to central corridor.

46. Bedroom reserved for additional crew accompanying he Ladyship on the yacht. Parker's room is on the port side of the central corridor.

47. Starboard gas turbine.

48. High-compression pump removes water from FAB 1's garage once the rear doors have closed.

49. Starboard magneto-hydro-dynamic aquajet.

50. Rear door hydraulics system.

51. Rear starboard FAB 1 docking clamp. Built-in shock absorbers prevent vehicle movement and damage in adverse weather conditions.

52. Watertight garage door and ramp. Using its hydrofoils, FAB 1 can dock with FAB 2 by steering into the yacht's garage. Once clamped in position, the garage door is closed and FAB 1's hydrofoils retract as water is pumped from the garage.

Since answering its first distress call, International Rescue has carried out an incredible number of rescue missions around the world and saved countless lives. Many of these missions are available to agents as vide-recordings, allowing them to view the methods and techniques used to effect a wide range of rescues in usually dangerous and extreme circumstances. This data store lists the mission recordings available, with information about personnel involved, equipment used and lives saved.

> **WARNING: Agents may wish to access copies of vide-recordings before consulting these mission files as they reveal classified information about operational procedures.**

MISSION CODE NAME
Alias Mr. Hackenbacker

DANGER ZONE: Airspace above Northern Europe

NOTIFICATION PROCESS: Emergency alarm signal transmitted by London Agent

GROUNDS FOR ACTION: High altitude attempt to hi-jack haute couture collection endangering passengers and crew of prototype aircraft

MISSION OPERATIVES: Scott Tracy, Virgil Tracy, Alan Tracy

EQUIPMENT DEPLOYED: Thunderbird 1, Thunderbird 2

MISSION REPORT: Under instructions from Brains, Thunderbird 2 launches dummy missile attack on hi-jacked aircraft forcing hi-jackers to abandon attempts to land aircraft at remote airstrip. Aircraft returns to original flight path to make assisted emergency landing at London Airport. Thunderbird 2 diverted to desert to despatch desperate criminal accomplices.

LIVES SAVED: Potentially endangered passengers and crew of hi-jacked aircraft

MISSION CODE NAME
Atlantic Inferno Incident 1

DANGER ZONE: Atlantic Ocean

NOTIFICATION PROCESS: Monitoring of alarm call by Thunderbird 5

GROUNDS FOR ACTION: Ignited gas leak considered potential hazard by acting controller of International Rescue

MISSION OPERATIVES: Virgil Tracy, Alan Tracy, Gordon Tracy

EQUIPMENT DEPLOYED: Thunderbird 1, Thunderbird 2, Thunderbird 4, Thunderbird 5, Mobile Control Unit, Remote Controlled Sealing Device

MISSION REPORT: Rogue experimental World Navy atomic gyropedo detonates on sea bed fracturing surface above gas field. Gas ignites in vicinity of Seascape drilling rig. Thunderbirds 1 and 2 despatched to area. Thunderbird 4 launched to install sub-aqua sealing cap. Leaking gas successfully contained.

LIVES SAVED: No direct risk to life

MISSION CODE NAME
Atlantic Inferno Incident 2

DANGER ZONE: Seascape Rig, Atlantic Ocean

NOTIFICATION PROCESS: Request for assistance from danger zone (initially rejected by acting controller of International Rescue)

GROUNDS FOR ACTION: Two rig technicians trapped in inspection capsule at base of rig.

MISSION OPERATIVES: Virgil Tracy, Alan Tracy, Gordon Tracy

EQUIPMENT DEPLOYED: Thunderbird 1, Thunderbird 2, Thunderbird 4, Thunderbird 5

MISSION REPORT: Explosive ignition of multiple gas field fractures in vicinity of Seascape rig creates oceanic wave damaging rig support leg. Inspection team trapped on sea bed in inspection capsule following partial collapse of leg. Thunderbirds 1 and 2 despatched to area and Thunderbird 4 launched to release inspection capsule from fouled cables and debris, prior to raising to surface with magnetic clamps. Thunderbird 2 airlifts capsule from danger zone.

LIVES SAVED: Two rig technicians

MISSION CODE NAME
Attack of the Alligators

DANGER ZONE: Ambro River, South America

NOTIFICATION PROCESS: Request for assistance from danger zone

GROUNDS FOR ACTION: Occupants of research facility threatened by genetically enhanced alligators

MISSION OPERATIVES: Scott Tracy, Virgil Tracy, Alan Tracy, Gordon Tracy,

EQUIPMENT DEPLOYED: Thunderbird 1, Thunderbird 2, Thunderbird 4, Thunderbird 5, Hoverjets, Tranquiliser gun

MISSION REPORT: Careless disposal of experimental formula during theft at research base results in creation of super-sized amphibians. On arrival at danger zone Scott gains entry to besieged building and co-ordinates rescue attempt. Creatures in vicinity of house tranquilised by Alan and Gordon, Alan luring one monstrous reptile from area at great personal risk. Subsequent escape of disreputable boatman with phial of formula leads to attack by remaining un-sedated creature. Phial recovered intact by Gordon following capsize of boatman's craft.

LIVES SAVED: Occupants of research base

MISSION CODE NAME
Brink of Disaster

DANGER ZONE: Pacific Atlantic Monorail, U.S.A.

NOTIFICATION PROCESS: Request for assistance from endangered vehicle

GROUNDS FOR ACTION: International Rescue chief trapped with Brains, Tin-Tin and company chairman aboard mono-train approaching structurally compromised section of track

MISSION OPERATIVES: Scott Tracy, Virgil Tracy

EQUIPMENT DEPLOYED: Thunderbird 1, Thunderbird 2, Thunderbird 5, Mechanical Grabs

MISSION REPORT: Damage to bridge girder support caused by crash of patrol heli-jet hit by lightning strike results in failure of electronic mono-railroad safety system, imperilling approaching high speed express on demonstration test run. Members of International Rescue team aboard train attempt to manually activate braking system but are unable to do so before train reaches bridge. Thunderbirds 1 and 2 arrive at danger zone as bridge structure buckles under weight of train. Electro-magnetic grabs utilised by Thunderbird 2 to airlift carriage to safety.

LIVES SAVED: Jeff Tracy, Tin-Tin, Brains, Warren Grafton

MISSION CODE NAME
The Cham-Cham

DANGER ZONE: Swiss Alps and Maxwell Field Airbase

NOTIFICATION PROCESS: Observation by Alan Tracy of link between live popular music broadcasts and rocket transporter crashes

GROUNDS FOR ACTION: Prevention of further rocket transporter crashes

MISSION OPERATIVES: Scott Tracy, Virgil Tracy, Alan Tracy, Tin-Tin, Lady Penelope Creighton-Ward, Parker

EQUIPMENT DEPLOYED: Thunderbird 1, Thunderbird 2

MISSION REPORT: London Agent sent on undercover mission to Alpine resort to investigate suspected covert anti-aircraft broadcasts. Musical arranger discovered to be encoding live performances of popular jazz quintet with classified rocket transporter flight plans. Re-vocalising of suspect transmission by London Agent diverts hostile enemy fighters. Thunderbird 2 deployed to assist field agents when escape route severed by enemy agent.

LIVES SAVED: Lady Penelope Creighton-Ward, Tin-Tin, Parker

MISSION CODE NAME
City of Fire

DANGER ZONE: Thompson Tower complex, North America

NOTIFICATION PROCESS: Request for assistance from danger zone site authorities

GROUNDS FOR ACTION: Family trapped in sealed sub-basement access corridor

MISSION OPERATIVES: Scott Tracy, Virgil Tracy

EQUIPMENT DEPLOYED: Thunderbird 1, Thunderbird 2, Thunderbird 5, Mobile Control Unit, Hoverjets, Oxyhydnite Cutting Equipment

MISSION REPORT: Disastrous sequence of events involving unskilled driver, failure of safety equipment, and lack of store room monitoring causes family to become trapped beneath structurally unsafe super tower. Following catastrophic collapse of structure optimum rescue solution formulated on site by critical path analysis proposes rubble clearance by Firefly preceding excavation by Mole to gain entry to corridor system. Calculated risk assessment by Scott authorises utilisation of Oxyhydnite cutting equipment to cut through series of safety doors to free trapped family.

LIVES SAVED: Joe, Blanche, and Tommy Carter

MISSION CODE NAME
Cry Wolf Incident 1

DANGER ZONE: Mountain range near Charity Springs, Australia

NOTIFICATION PROCESS: Request for assistance from danger zone

GROUNDS FOR ACTION: Boy trapped on crumbling mountain ledge

MISSION OPERATIVES: Scott Tracy

EQUIPMENT DEPLOYED: Thunderbird 1, Thunderbird 5

MISSION REPORT: On arrival at danger zone distress call found to have been transmitted as part of child's game. Father of boys assumes responsibility and apologises. Scott offers to arrange trip to Tracy Island to demonstrate serious consequences of hoax calls. Request accepted.

LIVES SAVED: None endangered

ADDITIONAL INFORMATION: Boys transported to Tracy Island under strict blackout conditions and given tour of installations. Security risk believed to minimal. Father advised to limit boys' use of radio equipment..

MISSION CODE NAME
Cry Wolf Incident 2

DANGER ZONE: Abandoned mine workings near Charity Springs, Australia

NOTIFICATION PROCESS: Distress call received from trapped boys. (believed to be hoax). Genuine nature of distress call confirmed by report from Satellite H.Q.

GROUNDS FOR ACTION: Boys trapped in derelict mine

MISSION OPERATIVES: Scott Tracy, Virgil Tracy, Alan Tracy

EQUIPMENT DEPLOYED: Thunderbird 1, Thunderbird 2, Thunderbird 5, Hoverjet, Portable Winch Unit

MISSION REPORT: Guided by radio signal transmissions Virgil and Alan gain entry to mine workings via vertical shaft and locate trapped boys beneath debris in blast damaged section. Boys freed as shaft roof collapses. Intruder responsible for trapping boys pursued by Scott until vehicle leaves road enabling retrieval of stolen surveillance satellite images from wreckage.

LIVES SAVED: Tony and Bob Williams

MISSION CODE NAME
Danger at Ocean Deep Incident 1

DANGER ZONE: Island of Ohwahu

NOTIFICATION PROCESS: Request for assistance from danger zone

GROUNDS FOR ACTION: Typhoon in area endangers hospital

MISSION OPERATIVES: Scott Tracy, Virgil Tracy, Gordon Tracy,

EQUIPMENT DEPLOYED: Thunderbird 1, Thunderbird 2, Hydro-Stats

MISSION REPORT: On arrival at danger zone, operation carried out to stabilise foundations of storm damaged hospital with aid of Hydro-Stats. Mission team fail to prevent collapse of isolation ward, but ward fortunately unoccupied.

LIVES SAVED: Occupants of hospital

ADDITIONAL INFORMATION: Transmissions routed via Thunderbird 5 disrupted by interference leading to communications black-out. Brains accompanies Alan to space station to monitor and record interference patterns. Brains to investigate possible causes of communication failure and prepare report.

MISSION CODE NAME
Danger at Ocean Deep Incident 2

DANGER ZONE: Mediterranean Ocean

NOTIFICATION PROCESS: Calculated risk assessment by International Rescue chief following scientific demonstration.

GROUNDS FOR ACTION: Crew of super tanker potentially endangered

MISSION OPERATIVES: Scott Tracy, Virgil Tracy, John Tracy,

EQUIPMENT DEPLOYED: Thunderbird 1, Thunderbird 2, Anti-radiation suits, laser cutters

MISSION REPORT: Demonstration of toxic chemical reaction leads to request for London Agent to investigate possible locations of OD60 sea-fungi. Report of presence in Mediterranean triggers launch of Thunderbird 1 and 2 to investigate potential danger to tanker transporting liquid Alsterene. Creation of electrostatic sea mist disables ship's power system, trapping crew in anti-radiation cabin with inoperative air supply unit. Scott and John board ship to release crew. Crew winched to safety aboard Thunderbird 2. Thunderbirds 1 and 2 depart area immediately prior to explosive destruction of vessel.

LIVES SAVED: Crew of Ocean Pioneer II

MISSION CODE NAME
Day of Disaster

DANGER ZONE: Allington Suspension Bridge, England

NOTIFICATION PROCESS: Danger zone alert from Brains following observation of site controlled rescue operation

GROUNDS FOR ACTION: Technicians trapped in nosecone of submerged automatically launch activated rocket

MISSION OPERATIVES: Scott Tracy, Virgil Tracy, Gordon Tracy, Brains, Lady Penelope Creighton-Ward, Parker

EQUIPMENT DEPLOYED: Thunderbird 1, Thunderbird 2, Thunderbird 4, Fab 1

MISSION REPORT: Following severe electrical storm, suspension bridge collapses while Martian Space Probe rocket convoy in transit. Up-ending of rocket into launch position on river bed activates onboard launch system, endangering technicians in nosecone. Thunderbirds 2 and 4 deployed to clear debris surrounding rocket nosecone and detach from main body for transportation to safety.

LIVES SAVED: Two Martian Space Probe rocket technicians

MISSION CODE NAME
Desperate Intruder

DANGER ZONE: Lake Anasta, North Africa

NOTIFICATION PROCESS: Expedition site tri-circuit radio contact broken

GROUNDS FOR ACTION: Investigation of cause of above failure of communication link

MISSION OPERATIVES: Scott Tracy, Virgil Tracy, Gordon Tracy

EQUIPMENT DEPLOYED: Thunderbird 1, Thunderbird 2, Thunderbird 4, Hydro-static Lifting Equipment

MISSION REPORT: Responding to emergency alarm, Thunderbirds 1 and 2 arrive at expedition base camp to discover Brains interred in sand, Tin-Tin comatose and archaeological advisor with head injuries. During later unsupervised survey of submerged temple, mysterious intruder induces mental blackout in Brains before triggering demolition of temple, trapping him beneath rubble. Thunderbird 4 launched to investigate explosion. After engaging in battle with hostile submarine, Thunderbird 4 locates Brains. Scott and Gordon deploy hydro-static lifting equipment to extricate Brains from debris.

LIVES SAVED: Brains, Tin-Tin, Professor Blakely

MISSION CODE NAME
The Duchess Assignment

DANGER ZONE: Abandoned house outside New York

NOTIFICATION PROCESS: Alarm raised by London Agent while monitoring satellite tracking

GROUNDS FOR ACTION: Disappearance of elderly aristocrat at New York air terminal

MISSION OPERATIVES: Scott Tracy, Virgil Tracy, Lady Penelope Creighton-Ward

EQUIPMENT DEPLOYED: Thunderbird 1, Thunderbird 2, Thunderbird 5, Fab 1, Mole, Restraining Unit (DOMO)

MISSION REPORT: Signal of homing transmitter planted on potentially endangered duchess traced to isolated house by Thunderbird 5. On arrival at transmission area signal source pinpointed to basement of combusting building by Thunderbird 1. Lack of fire fighting equipment aboard Thunderbird 2 due to insufficient danger zone data leads to rescue attempt carried out by Virgil using Mole. Scott provides additional mission support by deploying restraining unit to prevent potential structural damage to basement from collapse of unstable wall.

LIVES SAVED: Deborah, Duchess of Royston

MISSION CODE NAME
Edge of Impact

DANGER ZONE: Telecommunications Relay Tower, England

NOTIFICATION PROCESS: Monitoring of suspected test flight sabotage by Thunderbird 5

GROUNDS FOR ACTION: Men trapped in control room of damaged transmitter tower

MISSION OPERATIVES: Scott Tracy, Virgil Tracy, Alan Tracy,

EQUIPMENT DEPLOYED: Thunderbird 1, Thunderbird 2, Thunderbird 5, Remote Camera, Booster Mortar, Low Altitude Escape Harness

MISSION REPORT: Due to support stanchion damage sustained by impact of crash landing aircraft, two technicians trapped in control room of tele-relay tower. Following remote camera survey at danger zone by Thunderbird 1, Escape capsules fired into tower control room by booster mortar. Technicians engage jet pack thrusters to effect last minute escape as tower collapses.

LIVES SAVED: Two telecommunications technicians

MISSION CODE NAME
End of the Road

DANGER ZONE: South East Asia

NOTIFICATION PROCESS: Request for assistance from danger zone.

GROUNDS FOR ACTION: Man trapped in precariously balanced explosives tractor on unstable mountain ledge.

MISSION OPERATIVES: Scott Tracy, Virgil Tracy, Alan Tracy,

EQUIPMENT DEPLOYED: Thunderbird 1, Thunderbird 2, Thunderbird 5, Mechanical Grabs

MISSION REPORT: Attempt by construction company partner to secure road project by explosive demolition of mountain peak results in hazardous immobilisation of his vehicle. On arrival at danger zone Thunderbird 1 installs shield of impact absorbent spears to protect vehicle from dislodgement by falling debris. Following failure of initial attempts to secure and remove vehicle by Thunderbird 2 with aid of mechanical grabs, Thunderbird 1 deployed to provide practical operational support. Although rescued vehicle destroyed due to insufficient grip of mechanical grabs, occupant able to escape to terra firma.

LIVES SAVED: Eddie Houseman

MISSION CODE NAME
Give or Take a Million

DANGER ZONE: Coralville Hospital, North America

NOTIFICATION PROCESS: Request for assistance from hospital administrators

GROUNDS FOR ACTION: To provide special Christmas treat for disadvantaged youngster

MISSION OPERATIVES: Virgil Tracy,

EQUIPMENT DEPLOYED: Thunderbird 2,

MISSION REPORT: In joint venture with Coralville Hospital and Harman's department store, Christmas visit to Tracy island offered to deserving child. Lucky ticket to be concealed in seasonal gift for despatch by Christmas rocket. On delivery rocket payload discovered to contain unexpected Christmas bonus of two fugitive bank robbers. Thunderbird 2 transports lucky winner to Tracy Island for seasonal festivities.

LIVES SAVED: None endangered

ADDITIONAL INFORMATION: Remind Kyrano to check next year's calendar for printing errors.

MISSION CODE NAME
The Impostors

DANGER ZONE: South Pacific space observation quadrant

NOTIFICATION PROCESS: Monitoring of Space Observation Satellite

GROUNDS FOR ACTION: Astronaut adrift in space

MISSION OPERATIVES: Scott Tracy, Alan Tracy, Lady Penelope Creighton-Ward, Parker

EQUIPMENT DEPLOYED: Thunderbird 3, Thunderbird 5,

MISSION REPORT: Thunderbird 3 launched to perform space rescue mission following reports of astronaut jet pack malfunction. Astronaut safely located and returned to satellite.

LIVES SAVED: Satellite Operative Elliott

ADDITIONAL INFORMATION: Rescue mission launched despite danger of detection of International Rescue base by world security forces. Joint action by London and local agents results in capture of criminal imposters and undetected return of Thunderbird 3.

MISSION CODE NAME
Lord Parker's 'Oliday

DANGER ZONE: Monte Bianco, Italy

NOTIFICATION PROCESS: Warning of potentially great disaster by London Agent

GROUNDS FOR ACTION: Dislocated reflective energy collection dish threatens local town with solar generated incineration

MISSION OPERATIVES: Scott Tracy, Virgil Tracy, Alan Tracy, Brains

EQUIPMENT DEPLOYED: Thunderbird 1, Thunderbird 2

MISSION REPORT: Operation to make safe dangerously positioned wreckage of storm damaged solar generating station hampered by jammed mechanism of ray collection dish control system. Brains winched into gear housing to assess damage and disengage seized components. Temporary protection to town from effect of reflected solar rays created by generation of smokescreen from Thunderbird 1. Attempts to reposition dish prove unsuccessful when wreckage slips down mountainside. Brains believed buried later reports himself safe and carries out adjustments to mechanism.

LIVES SAVED: Inhabitants of Monte Bianco

MISSION CODE NAME
The Man From M.I.5

DANGER ZONE: Monte Carlo

NOTIFICATION PROCESS: Request for assistance from world security forces

GROUNDS FOR ACTION: Theft of secret plans threatens safety of the world

MISSION OPERATIVES: Scott Tracy, Virgil Tracy, Gordon Tracy, Lady Penelope Creighton-Ward

EQUIPMENT DEPLOYED: Thunderbird 1, Thunderbird 2, Thunderbird 4, Thunderbird 5, Fab 1, Sonar Soundscan, Paralyser

MISSION REPORT: Assigned to locate stolen secret plans, London Agent poses as informant with inside knowledge of theft. Action results in capture of London Agent by gang leader and incarceration aboard booby-trapped motor cruiser. Thunderbirds 1 and 2 launched following transmission of coded distress signal. After locating criminal fugitives' submarine and disabling crew, London Agent released by Scott and secret plans recovered by Gordon.

LIVES SAVED: Lady Penelope Creighton-Ward

MISSION CODE NAME
Martian Invasion

DANGER ZONE: Nevada Desert, U.S.A.

NOTIFICATION PROCESS: Request for assistance from danger zone

GROUNDS FOR ACTION: Actors trapped in flooded cave due to pyrotechnic misuse

MISSION OPERATIVES: Scott Tracy, Virgil Tracy,

EQUIPMENT DEPLOYED: Thunderbird 1, Thunderbird 2, Thunderbird 5, Mobile Control Unit, Drilling and Crushing Excavator, Hoverjets

MISSION REPORT: On arrival at danger zone, Drilling and Crushing Excavator deployed to release endangered men. Following successful resolution of mission, incident proved to have been engineered deliberately by bogus film producer to record secrets of International Rescue. Thunderbirds 1 and 2 pursue impostor who attempts to effect escape by land and air. Pursuit abandoned when fugitive's aircraft discovered not to be airworthy.

LIVES SAVED: Two film actors

MISSION CODE NAME
The Mighty Atom

DANGER ZONE: Sahara Atomic Irrigation Plant

NOTIFICATION PROCESS: Request for assistance from danger zone site authorities

GROUNDS FOR ACTION: Co-ordinated emergency shut-down operation required to prevent explosion of nuclear reactor

MISSION OPERATIVES: Scott Tracy, Virgil Tracy, Gordon Tracy, Lady Penelope Creighton-Ward (observational duties only)

EQUIPMENT DEPLOYED: Thunderbird 1, Thunderbird 2, Thunderbird 4, Thunderbird 5, Mobile Control Unit

MISSION REPORT: Deliberate attempt to destroy atomic irrigation plant leads to imminent risk of atomic disaster. Scott and Virgil carry out shutdown procedure in reactor control chamber timed in phase with missile detonated de-activation of sea-water intake by Thunderbird 4.

LIVES SAVED: Staff of atomic plant and potentially endangered local population

MISSION CODE NAME
Move and You're Dead

DANGER ZONE: Bridge of San Miguel, New Mexico

NOTIFICATION PROCESS: Wrist tele-call alert from Alan Tracy

GROUNDS FOR ACTION: Alan Tracy and Grandma trapped on booby-trapped bridge

MISSION OPERATIVES: Scott Tracy, Virgil Tracy, Brains,

EQUIPMENT DEPLOYED: Thunderbird 1, Thunderbird 2, Neutraliser Tractor, Jet-air Transporter

MISSION REPORT: After performance proving test drive by Alan in Parola Sands Grand Prix, experimentally powered BR2 sports car built by Brains stolen in highway robbery by reckless rival racing team. Alan Tracy and Grandma left stranded on girder of newly completed canyon bridge in close proximity to sonic wave device primed to detonate bomb on underside of bridge on detection of slightest movement. Virgil and Brains utilise Neutraliser Tractor and Jet-Air Transporter to effect rescue.

LIVES SAVED: Grandma and Alan Tracy

MISSION CODE NAME
Operation Crash Dive Incident 1

DANGER ZONE: Atlantic Ocean Sea Bed 180 miles NW of TS749/AP428

NOTIFICATION PROCESS: Alert from Thunderbird 5 while monitoring Fireflash flight

GROUNDS FOR ACTION: Two man crew believed trapped in aircraft on seabed

MISSION OPERATIVES: Scott Tracy, Virgil Tracy, Gordon Tracy, Brains

EQUIPMENT DEPLOYED: Thunderbird 1, Thunderbird 2, Thunderbird 4, Thunderbird 5, Mobile Control Unit, Mobile Electronic Scanner, Light-type

MISSION REPORT: Failure of EPU aboard Fireflash during test flight causes aircraft to crash into the Atlantic. Electronic scanning of area from Mobile Control position reveals no trace of aircraft on ocean surface. Following search by Thunderbird 4 aircraft located intact on sea bed. Acting on advice from Brains, tailplane mounted engine units dismantled allowing aircraft to float to surface. Crew released from cabin and airlifted to safety by Thunderbird 2 before electrical fire causes aircraft to explode.

LIVES SAVED: Fireflash test crew

MISSION CODE NAME
Operation Crash Dive Incident 2

DANGER ZONE: Airspace above Atlantic Ocean 20 miles NW of LS749/AP428

NOTIFICATION PROCESS: Mission carried out on suggestion of International Rescue

GROUNDS FOR ACTION: Attempt to determine cause of Fireflash crashes, and prevent further similar incidents

MISSION OPERATIVES: Scott Tracy, Virgil Tracy, Gordon Tracy,

EQUIPMENT DEPLOYED: Thunderbird 2, Thunderbird 5, Air to Air Rescue Equipment, (Diving Escape Bell loaded but not required)

MISSION REPORT: Supervision of test flight results in detection of ruthless professional saboteur by Gordon after mid-air boarding of aircraft wing section to investigate EPU failure. Following gun battle saboteur falls from aircraft. Gordon renders EPU temporarily operational enabling crew to regain control of aircraft.

LIVES SAVED: Scott Tracy, Captain Hanson

MISSION CODE NAME
Path of Destruction

DANGER ZONE: San Martino, South America

NOTIFICATION PROCESS: Request for assistance from danger zone

GROUNDS FOR ACTION: Rogue Crablogger deforestation processor threatens disaster

MISSION OPERATIVES: Scott Tracy, Virgil Tracy, Brains, Lady Penelope Creighton-Ward, Parker

EQUIPMENT DEPLOYED: Thunderbird 1, Thunderbird 2, Thunderbird 5, Fab 1, Crane

MISSION REPORT: Food poisoning results in collapse of two man crew of semi-automated nuclear powered logging leviathan. Machine subsequently runs off course threatening destruction of nearby town and newly completed dam. Rescue mission launched and operation successfully mounted at danger zone to board Crablogger and retrieve stricken crew. Danger zone action initiated by Scott to drain potentially hazardous Superon fuel from vehicle on completion of successful reactor shut-down reduces damage from unavoidable destruction following fall from cliff-side track.

LIVES SAVED: Two man crew of Crablogger and innumerable lives in local area.

MISSION CODE NAME
The Perils of Penelope

DANGER ZONE: Anderbad, Switzerland

NOTIFICATION PROCESS: Request from industrialist associate of International Rescue

GROUNDS FOR ACTION: Investigation required into unexplained disappearance of research scientist from non-stop mono-train.

MISSION OPERATIVES: Virgil Tracy, Alan Tracy, Gordon Tracy, Lady Penelope, Parker

EQUIPMENT DEPLOYED: Thunderbird 2, Monobrake

MISSION REPORT: London Agent and Sir Jeremy Hodge carry out on-board enquiries into disappearance of Professor Borender from Transcontinental Rocket, Thunderbird 2 launched to monitor Anderbad terminus. Following arrival of service Parker reports London Agent and companion no longer among passengers. Virgil and Gordon enter tunnel aboard Monobrake to conduct a search. Industrial espionage agent's base discovered.Virgil and Gordon force surrender of criminal mastermind and facilitate escape of London Agent from perilous trap.

LIVES SAVED: Lady Penelope Creighton-Ward, Sir Jeremy Hodge, Professor Borender

MISSION CODE NAME
Pit of Peril

DANGER ZONE: Africa (exact location classified)

NOTIFICATION PROCESS: Monitoring of World Army experimental field trials by Thunderbird 5

GROUNDS FOR ACTION: Crew of Sidewinder class Jungle Cat transporter trapped when vehicle falls into self-combusting arms cache.

MISSION OPERATIVES: Scott Tracy, Virgil Tracy, Brains

EQUIPMENT DEPLOYED: Thunderbird 1, Thunderbird 2, Thunderbird 5, Remote Camera, Mobile Control Unit, Mole, Master Recovery Vehicle, Remote Control Recovery Vehicle

MISSION REPORT: Subsidence of ground above burning buried armaments disposal area traps crew of giant mechanical quadruped in hostile environment 300 feet below surface. Following on site recommendations by Brains, Virgil is lowered into rescue area to plant charges to remove unstable topsoil overhang. Virgil collected from detonation area by Scott in Mole. On successful detonation of charges, recovery vehicles equipped with high powered suction devices deployed to haul Sidewinder to surface.

LIVES SAVED: Three man crew of Sidewinder

MISSION CODE NAME
Ricochet

DANGER ZONE: KLA satellite orbital path and A'Ben Du Oil Refinery

NOTIFICATION PROCESS: Request for assistance from unauthorised television broadcasting satellite

GROUNDS FOR ACTION: Two men trapped in damaged satellite on uncontrolled decaying orbital descent

MISSION OPERATIVES: Scott Tracy, Virgil Tracy, Alan Tracy, Brains,

EQUIPMENT DEPLOYED: Thunderbird 2, Thunderbird 3,

MISSION REPORT: Thunderbird 3 launched to effect orbital rescue of trapped satellite occupants. Alan forced to resort to extreme methods of persuasion when one satellite occupant expresses reluctance to don spacesuit. Additional rescue support provided by Thunderbird 2 to prevent potentially disastrous crash-landing of satellite on oil refinery.

LIVES SAVED: Rick O'Shay, Loman, workers at A'Ben Du oil refinery.

MISSION CODE NAME
Security Hazard

DANGER ZONE: Northern England

NOTIFICATION PROCESS: Request for assistance from danger zone

GROUNDS FOR ACTION: Rescue of men trapped in shaft beneath blazing mine

MISSION OPERATIVES: Scott Tracy, Virgil Tracy

EQUIPMENT DEPLOYED: Thunderbird 1, Thunderbird 2, Fire-Cat

MISSION REPORT: After successful completion of rescue operation Thunderbird 2 returns to base with fault in electrical system. Resulting failure of on-board security monitors found to have compromised base security when small boy concealed in pod triggers hangar intruder detectors. Decision taken to rely on improbability of any account boy might make of visit to maintain cover.

LIVES SAVED: Men trapped in mine shaft.

MISSION CODE NAME
Sun Probe

DANGER ZONE: Solar Space Quadrant

NOTIFICATION PROCESS: Request for assistance from solar mission control anticipated by warning from Brains

GROUNDS FOR ACTION: Due to malfunction, manned solar probe rocket drawn into gravitational pull of the sun

MISSION OPERATIVES: Scott Tracy, Virgil Tracy, Alan Tracy, Brains Tin-Tin,

EQUIPMENT DEPLOYED: Thunderbird 2, Thunderbird 3, Transmitter Truck, Braman

MISSION REPORT: Joint mission by Thunderbird 2 and 3 launched to save crew of Sun Probe rocket. Attempts by Thunderbird 3 to over-ride malfunctioning Sun Probe retro-rocket controls with radio beam eventually successful, but power drain renders Thunderbird 3 retro-rocket control system inoperative. Back-up mission supervised by Brains at Mount Arkan enables crucial transmission of trans-spatial impulse beam to restore Thunderbird 3 systems.

LIVES SAVED: Solarnauts Asher, Camp and Harris, and during course of rescue, Scott Tracy, Alan Tracy and Tin-Tin

MISSION FILES

MISSION CODE NAME
Terror In New York City Incident 1

DANGER ZONE: Middle Eastern Oilfield

NOTIFICATION PROCESS: Offer of assistance from International Rescue

GROUNDS FOR ACTION: Oil well flare up threatens environmental disaster and provides opportunity to test Firefly.

MISSION OPERATIVES: Scott Tracy, Virgil Tracy

EQUIPMENT DEPLOYED: Thunderbird 1, Thunderbird 2, Firefly

MISSION REPORT: Oil field fire successfully extinguished in test exercise by Firefly. Scott prevents potential security breach by electromagnetically wiping news crew's recording of Thunderbird 1 departure.

LIVES SAVED: None immediately at risk.

ADDITIONAL INFORMATION: During return to base, Thunderbird 2 mistakenly attacked by USN strike vessel and sustains damage following failure of jammers. Emergency crash landing procedures fail to prevent further damage on touch-down. Craft withdrawn from service while repairs effected.

MISSION CODE NAME
Terror In New York City Incident 2

DANGER ZONE: New York City

NOTIFICATION PROCESS: Offer of assistance from International Rescue

GROUNDS FOR ACTION: News reporter and cameraman trapped in flood threatened cavern beneath collapsed New York landmark.

MISSION OPERATIVES: Scott Tracy, Gordon Tracy

EQUIPMENT DEPLOYED: Thunderbird 1, Thunderbird 4, Mobile Control Unit

MISSION REPORT: Attempted relocation of Empire State Building results in disaster when inadequate survey fails to model potentially catastrophic results of ground subsidence. Subsequent collapse of building traps film crew beneath water level in subterranean cavern. Thunderbird 1 launched to supervise rescue mission from danger zone. Due to non-operational status of Thunderbird 2, Thunderbird 4 delivered to danger zone by US Navy. Thunderbird 4 negotiates underground river system to locate trapped men.

LIVES SAVED: Reporter Ned Cook and cameraman.

MISSION CODE NAME
Thirty Minutes After Noon Incident 1

DANGER ZONE: Hudson Building, Spoke City

NOTIFICATION PROCESS: Request for assistance from danger zone

GROUNDS FOR ACTION: Man trapped at bottom of elevator shaft in burning building

MISSION OPERATIVES: Scott Tracy, Virgil Tracy, Alan Tracy,

EQUIPMENT DEPLOYED: Thunderbird 1, Thunderbird 2, Thunderbird 5, Mobile Control Unit, Dicetylene Cage

MISSION REPORT: Member of international criminal gang forces Hudson Building employee to destroy files by planting wrist-lock incendiary device in building. Employee trapped in sub-basement during attempt to exit building due to elevator cable breakage. On arrival at danger zone, Virgil and Alan install and operate Dicetylene Cage to successfully carry out rescue.

LIVES SAVED: Tom Prescott

MISSION CODE NAME
Thirty Minutes After Noon Incident 2

DANGER ZONE: British Atomic Centre, North of England

NOTIFICATION PROCESS: Request for assistance from British security services

GROUNDS FOR ACTION: Intelligence agent held by security robot in sealed atomic centre vault containing timed explosive devices.

MISSION OPERATIVES: Scott Tracy, Virgil Tracy, Lady Penelope Creighton-Ward, Parker

EQUIPMENT DEPLOYED: Thunderbird 1, Thunderbird 2, Thunderbird 5, Fab 1, Laser Beam Equipment

MISSION REPORT: Access to atomic centre vault area through disabled electronic doors achieved by Scott and Virgil with aid of laser beam equipment. Robot security guard deactivated to free trapped undercover operative. Explosive charges disposed of at sea by Thunderbird 1 immediately prior to detonation.

LIVES SAVED: British Intelligence agent Southern, local population at risk from nuclear detonation

MISSION CODE NAME
Trapped in the Sky

DANGER ZONE: London International Airport, England

NOTIFICATION PROCESS: Automatic distress signal monitoring aboard Thunderbird 5

GROUNDS FOR ACTION: Sabotage of atomic powered airliner

MISSION OPERATIVES: Scott Tracy, Virgil Tracy, Lady Penelope Creighton-Ward, Parker

EQUIPMENT DEPLOYED: Thunderbird 1, Thunderbird 2, Thunderbird 5, Fab 1, Mobile Control Unit, Elevator Cars

MISSION REPORT: Sabotage by persons unknown endangers lives aboard airliner. Aircraft's inability to land due to explosive device placed in landing gear subjects passengers and crew to potential danger of radiation hazard on expiration of reactor safety factor. Mission successfully accomplished with aid of high speed mobile elevator cars. On activation of Thunderbird 1 ACD during rescue, London Agent alerted to deal with potential security risk.

LIVES SAVED: Crew and 600 passengers of Fireflash aircraft, including International Rescue team member Tin-Tin Kyrano.

MISSION CODE NAME
The Uninvited Incident 1

DANGER ZONE: The Sahara Desert

NOTIFICATION PROCESS: Report received from archaeological survey expedition

GROUNDS FOR ACTION: Thunderbird 1 and pilot require recovery after hostile action results in crash-landing

MISSION OPERATIVES: Virgil Tracy, Brains, Tin-Tin

EQUIPMENT DEPLOYED: Thunderbird 2, Thunderbird 5

MISSION REPORT: Attack reported against Thunderbird 1 while returning from mission over North Africa. Craft sustains tail unit damage and forced to crash-land. Due to injuries and communication equipment failure Scott unable to report position. Fortunate discovery by archaeological survey team provides essential location fix to facilitate recovery operation by Thunderbird 2. Brains carries out crash site repairs enabling Thunderbird 1 to return to base for full systems check.

LIVES SAVED: None immediately at risk. Scott to undergo check-up.

MISSION CODE NAME
The Uninvited Incident 2

DANGER ZONE: Lost Pyramid of Khamandides

NOTIFICATION PROCESS: Request for assistance from danger zone

GROUNDS FOR ACTION: Archaeological expedition stranded in desert

MISSION OPERATIVES: Scott Tracy, Virgil Tracy, Gordon Tracy

EQUIPMENT DEPLOYED: Thunderbird 1, Thunderbird 2, Thunderbird 5,

MISSION REPORT: Abandoned archaeologists transport located in vicinity of legendary long lost pyramid. After discovery of secret entrance to structure, Scott becomes trapped inside with archaeologists by race of technologically advanced pyramid dwellers. Pyramid found to be base for fighters responsible for earlier attack on Thunderbird 1. Decisive action by Scott enables captive party to escape as attack launched against Thunderbird 2. Internal fuel storage safety systems failure results in massive explosive destruction of pyramid.

LIVES SAVED: Archaeological survey team. Occupants of lost pyramid regretfully believed victims of ancient monument's destruction.

MISSION CODE NAME
Vault of Death

DANGER ZONE: Bank of England, London

NOTIFICATION PROCESS: Request for assistance received from site authorities

GROUNDS FOR ACTION: Man trapped in automated vacuum fitted vault

MISSION OPERATIVES: Scott Tracy, Virgil Tracy, Alan Tracy, Lady Penelope Creighton-Ward, Parker

EQUIPMENT DEPLOYED: Thunderbird 1, Thunderbird 2, Thunderbird 5, Mobile Control Unit, The Mole (unusable due to local authority objections), Hoverjets

MISSION REPORT: As a result of clerical error, man trapped in automated high security bank vault fitted with vacuum assisted document preservation system. Attempts to cut through vault door with laser cutting equipment prove ineffective. Senior member of Tracy household suggests access route via abandoned underground transit network. Mission successful but deployment of equipment potentially superfluous as local agents arrive at scene to effect simultaneous rescue operation.

LIVES SAVED: Bank employee Lambert